Mentoring Children for Social Inclusion

Mentoring Children and Young People for Social Inclusion critically analyses the challenges and possibilities of mentoring approaches to youth welfare and equality. It explores existing youth mentoring programmes targeted towards youth in care, immigrant, and refugee populations, and considers the extent to which these can aid social inclusion.

The book compiles works by scholars from different countries focused on how child and youth mentoring has been changing globally in recent years and how these changes are identified and approached in different contexts. The book seeks to address what empowering youth means in different sociopolitical contexts, how mentoring is approached by governments and NGOs, and how these approaches shape mentoring relationships. It provides insights on how mentoring can tackle structural inequalities and work towards child and youth empowerment.

This book will be of great interest for academics, scholars, and postgraduate students in the area of inclusive education and mentoring. It will also be useful reading for social workers, community developers, and practitioners working in NGOs, as well as for governments looking for innovative ways to generate interventions in the educational and social arena.

Òscar Prieto-Flores is Associate Professor of Sociology at the University of Girona, Spain. He is currently Principal Investigator of *APPlying Mentoring*, a RECERCAIXA research grant gathering a team of 16 researchers from United States and Spanish universities.

Jordi Feu is Professor of Education Policy at the University of Girona, Spain. He is currently the head of the "Cabinet for Social Mentoring" of the University of Girona.

Mentoring Children and Young People for Social Inclusion

Global Approaches to Empowerment

Edited by
Òscar Prieto-Flores and Jordi Feu

LONDON AND NEW YORK

First published 2021
by Routledge
2 Park Square, Milton Park, Abingdon, Oxon OX14 4RN

and by Routledge
52 Vanderbilt Avenue, New York, NY 10017

Routledge is an imprint of the Taylor & Francis Group, an informa business

© 2021 selection and editorial matter, Òscar Prieto-Flores and Jordi Feu; individual chapters, the contributors

The right of Òscar Prieto-Flores and Jordi Feu to be identified as the authors of the editorial material, and of the authors for their individual chapters, has been asserted in accordance with sections 77 and 78 of the Copyright, Designs and Patents Act 1988.

All rights reserved. No part of this book may be reprinted or reproduced or utilised in any form or by any electronic, mechanical, or other means, now known or hereafter invented, including photocopying and recording, or in any information storage or retrieval system, without permission in writing from the publishers.

Trademark notice: Product or corporate names may be trademarks or registered trademarks, and are used only for identification and explanation without intent to infringe.

British Library Cataloguing-in-Publication Data
A catalogue record for this book is available from the British Library

Library of Congress Cataloging-in-Publication Data
A catalog record has been requested for this book

ISBN: 978-0-367-36431-1 (hbk)
ISBN: 978-0-429-34595-1 (ebk)

Typeset in Bembo
by Cenveo® Publisher Services

Contents

List of illustrations	vii
List of contributors	viii
Preface	xiv

1 **Critical autonomy, social capital, and mentoring programmes for children and youth**   1
 ÒSCAR PRIETO-FLORES, JORDI FEU, XAVIER CASADEMONT, AND XAVIER ALARCÓN

2 **The importance of being present: Mentors as "presence practitioners"**   16
 BERNADINE BRADY AND PAT DOLAN

3 **The role of mentoring and service learning in youth's critical consciousness and social change efforts**   32
 BERNADETTE SÁNCHEZ, BETH S. CATLETT, LIDIA Y. MONJARAS-GAYTAN, REBECCA MCGARITY-PALMER, AMY J. ANDERSON, C. LYNN LIAO, AND CHRISTOPHER B. KEYS

4 **New approaches to empower youth to recruit mentors in the United States**   47
 SARAH SCHWARTZ, MCKENNA PARNES, LAURA AUSTIN, AND REBECCA BROWNE

5 **Youth-Initiated Mentoring: Promoting and improving the social networks of youth with complex needs in the Netherlands**   64
 LEVI VAN DAM, ELLIS TER BEEK, AND NATASHA KOPER

6 **Youth mentoring and multiple social support attunement: Contributions to understand youth social development and well-being** 94
FRANCISCO SIMÕES, MARIA MANUELA CALHEIROS, AND MADALENA ALARCÃO

7 **The methodological issues in the assessment of quality and the benefits of formal youth mentoring interventions: The case of the Czech Big Brothers Big Sisters/Pět P** 110
TEREZA BRUMOVSKÁ AND GABRIELA SEIDLOVÁ MÁLKOVÁ

Conclusions 128

Index 133

Illustrations

Figures
5.1	The four phases of the YIM approach	71
6.1	Multiple social support attunement framework – graphical summary	103

Tables
1.1	The multilevel social capital framework for mentoring programmes	8
5.1	Rules of thumb for professionals to use the YIM approach effectively	85
7.1	Stages and themes in the dynamics of formal youth mentoring relationships	120

Contributors

Òscar Prieto-Flores is Associate Professor at the University of Girona. He obtained his PhD in Sociology from the University of Barcelona in 2007 and was Visiting Scholar in 2006 of the Center for Migration and Development at Princeton University, in 2012 of the Center for Comparative Studies in Race and Ethnicity at Stanford University, and in 2017 at the Center for Evidence-Based Mentoring at UMASS Boston. He is also Principal Investigator of the RECERCAIXA research project *APPLYING MENTORING: Social and Technological Innovations for the Inclusion of Immigrant and Refugee Populations (2018–2021)*.

Jordi Feu is Professor of Education Policy at the University of Girona. His scholarly work focuses on educational reform social movements, their influence on education policy, and how democratic participation and empowerment take place in different social and educational settings. He published recently in the journal, *Children and Youth Services Review*, on youth mentoring.

Xavier Casademont is Assistant Professor at the University of Girona and a political scientist. His PhD focuses on the process of integration of internal migration during the Franco regime. His main areas of interest are immigrant integration policies and citizenship, social policies, and social services, as well as the crisis of liberal democracies and political participation. He was a civil servant in a town council in Catalonia for 13 years, and acted as a coordinator of the immigrant plan.

Xavier Alarcón is a PhD candidate at the University of Girona. His research is focused on the transition to adulthood of former unaccompanied minors. His experience in the field of mentoring began working as a practitioner in the Nightingale mentoring programme. He also worked in the development of a mentoring programme led by the Catalan Government aiming the social inclusion of asylum seekers and refugees.

Bernadine Brady is Lecturer at the School of Political Science & Sociology, and a Senior Researcher with the UNESCO Child and Family Research

Centre at NUI, Galway. Brady is a mixed methods researcher with a focus on social ecology and young people's well-being, exploring how community, school, family, and service provision influence outcomes for young people. She has published a wide range of peer-reviewed journal articles, book chapters, and reports in relation to youth mentoring, participation, youth work, and empathy. She is co-author of *A Guide to Youth Mentoring: Providing Effective Social Support* (Jessica Kingsley, 2012, with Pat Dolan) and of *Mentoring Young People in Care and Leaving Care: Theory, Policy and Practice* (Routledge, 2020, with Pat Dolan and Caroline McGregor).

Pat Dolan is a Joint Founder and Director of the UNESCO Child and Family Research Centre at the National University of Ireland, Galway, and holds the prestigious UNESCO Chair in Children, Youth and Civic Engagement. The UNESCO Chair programme is built around core strands of research, teaching, policy advocacy, and practice and is underpinned by a range of national and international collaborations. Prof. Dolan has worked with and for families as a practitioner, service manager, and academic. He has published widely on empathy and civic engagement in children and youth, family support, reflective practice, youth mentoring, adolescent resilience, and social support. He is co-author of *A Guide to Youth Mentoring: Providing Effective Social Support* (Jessica Kingsley, 2012, with Bernadine Brady) and of *Mentoring Young People in Care and Leaving Care: Theory, Policy and Practice* (Routledge, 2020, with Bernadine Brady and Caroline McGregor).

Bernadette Sánchez is Professor of Community Psychology at DePaul University in Chicago, IL. She is an expert on the role of mentoring relationships in the positive development and education of urban, low-income adolescents of colour. Sánchez has authored literature reviews on the roles of race, ethnicity, and culture in youth mentoring for the leading scholarly handbook for youth mentoring, and she has over 50 publications and 120 presentations. She recently completed a Distinguished Fellowship Award with the William T. Grant Foundation. She has received funding from the National Institutes of Health (NIH), National Science Foundation (NSF), and local foundations for her mentoring research. Bernadette is a member of the Research Board for the National Mentoring Resource Center in the United States. She received her bachelor's degree in Psychology from Fairfield University, Fairfield, CT, and her master's and PhD degrees in Community and Prevention Research from the University of Illinois at Chicago, IL.

Beth S. Catlett is Associate Professor and Chair of the Department of Women's and Gender Studies at DePaul University, and Cofounder and Director of the Beck Research Initiative for Women, Gender, and Community that specialises in community-based research involving gendered violence and social movements to create community change. She also is the Director of the Faculty Scholarship Support Center in DePaul's College of Liberal Arts & Social Sciences. Dr. Catlett's areas of scholarly interest include youth leadership and activism, community-based participatory action research, violence in intimate relationships, and the uses of contemplative practices to inspire critical consciousness. Her research has been published in numerous books and journals, including *Violence Against Women*, *Men & Masculinities*, *American Journal of Community Psychology*, and *Michigan Journal of Community Service Learning*. Dr. Catlett also co-edited, with Dr. Michele Morano, *Write Your Heart Out: Chicagoland Teens on Relationships: An Interactive Anthology*.

Lidia Y. Monjaras-Gaytan is a third-year doctoral student in DePaul University's Community Psychology programme where her research focuses on mentoring and critical consciousness. She received her Bachelor of Arts in Psychology from San Diego State University in 2014 and completed her master's degree in Community Psychology at DePaul University in 2019.

Rebecca McGarity-Palmer is a third-year Community Psychology doctoral student at DePaul University. Her research centres around social justice, racial and gender equity, and access to healthcare. She received her Bachelor of Arts in Psychology from Houghton College in 2015 and completed her master's degree in Community Psychology at DePaul University in 2019.

Amy J. Anderson is a doctoral candidate in Community Psychology at DePaul University. Prior to doctoral study she was a middle school teacher and obtained her MS in Education from Johns Hopkins University. Her programme of research focuses on positive youth development, youth mentoring, and educational equity.

C. Lynn Liao is a Research Associate with Davis Pier Consulting, working primarily in Pier Labs, a social policy and innovation laboratory. She graduated from DePaul University with a PhD in Community Psychology in 2017 and has worked in research, evaluation, planning, and policy roles in Canadian government departments. Her most recent policy areas of interest include social assistance programmes such as income assistance and employment programmes for persons experiencing poverty, and housing assistance and homelessness interventions. She is currently the Principal Investigator on a longitudinal mixed methods research project (2020–2023) funded by the Canada Mortgage and Housing Corporation (CMHC) that will examine the role of housing subsidies in housing outcomes and quality of life for low-income households in Nova Scotia.

Christopher B. Keys is Professor Emeritus and former Chair of the Psychology Departments at DePaul University and the University of Illinois at Chicago, IL. Keys served as the Founding Associate Dean for Research in the College of Science and Health at DePaul and his research is focused on issues of empowerment among people with disabilities, especially people of colour. He co-edited the *Handbook of Community Psychology* and *Race, Culture and Disability Rehabilitation Science and Practice*. He recently co-authored the College Student Empowerment Scales for Racial/Ethnic Minorities in the *Journal of Community Psychology*. Keys has received the Distinguished Contribution to Theory and Research in Community Psychology Award from the Society for Community Research and Action. He has contributed about 150 peer-reviewed articles, chapters, and books and has presented his work on six continents.

Sarah Schwartz is Assistant Professor of Psychology at Suffolk University in Boston. She holds a doctorate in Clinical Psychology from the University of Massachusetts Boston and a master's degree in Education from the Harvard Graduate School of Education. Her research aims to develop, evaluate, and refine interventions that leverage the power of relationships to support the development of youth, with a particular emphasis on the role of mentoring relationships. She has published numerous articles and chapters on the topic and is the current recipient of a William T. Grant Foundation research grant to study an intervention designed to increase social capital and networks of support among first-generation college students.

McKenna Parnes is currently a doctoral student in Suffolk University's Clinical Psychology PhD programme. She received an MSEd degree in Counseling and Mental Health from the University of Pennsylvania in 2016. Her clinical and research interests are focused on supporting positive development in underrepresented youth and identifying strategies to promote youth access to supportive relationships.

Laura Austin is currently a doctoral student in Suffolk University's Clinical Psychology PhD programme, where she earned an MS in Clinical Psychology in 2019. Her clinical and research interests centre on empowering and supporting youth in their development and promoting youth help-seeking.

Rebecca Browne is currently a second-year doctoral student in Suffolk University's Clinical Psychology PhD programme. Her clinical and research interests focus on fostering positive youth development and resiliency, particularly in underrepresented youth.

Levi van Dam is Founder of the YIM foundation in the Netherlands and chairman of the board of Garage2020, an innovation network spread across the Netherlands. He obtained his PhD in forensic juvenile psychology at the University of Amsterdam in 2018 on Youth-Initiated Mentoring. He currently teaches at the University of Amsterdam and conducts research on innovation in youth care.

Ellis ter Beek is Director of treatment at Rosales Care. She obtained her PhD in forensic juvenile psychology from the University of Amsterdam in 2018, her research focused on treatment of juveniles with severe sexual problem behaviour. Since 1997 she has worked in Forensic Youth Care (FYC) and Secure Youth Care (SYC) institutions. She has many years of clinical expertise regarding juveniles with severely transgressive behaviour. Her personal area of interest is the comorbidity of psychiatric disorders, borderline intellectual functioning, and (forensic) behavioural problems in adolescents, focusing explicitly on the development of the juvenile in interaction with his/her context.

Natasha Koper is a PhD candidate at Utrecht University. She researches the effects of the Youth-Initiated Mentoring (YIM) approach as an outpatient alternative for out-of-home care for adolescents of multi-problem families. She is also the PhD representative of Child and Adolescent studies in the PhD Council of the Faculty of Social and Behavioural Sciences of Utrecht University.

Francisco Simões is Assistant Researcher and a full member of the Center for Social Research and Intervention at the University Institute of Lisbon (CIS-IUL). He currently co-coordinates the research group Community, Education and Development (CED) at CIS-IUL. He is also the Chair of the COST Action entitled Rural NEET Youth Network – Modeling, the risks underlying rural NEETs social exclusion. For the past 15 years he has been involved in several community- and school-based projects design, management, and assessment funded by public and private organisations in Portugal. His research interests cover topics such as adolescents' social development and well-being, social support, youth mentoring, or rural NEETs psychosocial profile. He has authored and co-authored various international peer-reviewed papers on these issues.

Maria Manuela Calheiros, PhD in Community Social Psychology from University Institute of Lisbon (ISCTE-IUL) 2003, is Associate Professor at the Faculty of Psychology, University of Lisbon, and the Principal Investigator of the CIRC research project – Social Images, organisational climate, and quality of relationships in Residential Care: The design, implementation, and evaluation of an intervention programme (2019–2022). From 2006 to 2013, she was the Coordinator of the Masters in Community Psychology and Child Protection; from 2010 to 2013, she was the President of the Portuguese Association of Psychology; as well as from 2012 to 2014, she was the President of the Department of Social and Organizational Psychology at ISCTE.

Madalena Alarcão is Associate Professor at the Faculty of Psychology and Education Sciences of the University of Coimbra. She obtained her PhD in Clinical Psychology from the University of Coimbra in 1991. She is a research member of the Center for Social Studies of the University of Coimbra. She is a family therapist and a supervisor member of the Portuguese Family Therapy Society. Embracing a systemic approach, she conducts research on issues of parental education, parenting skills, family violence, and social networks. She lectures in the field of systemic and family intervention in clinical and forensic settings.

Tereza Brumovská earned a PhD in Sociology (2017) from the UNESCO Child and Family Research Centre, School of Political Science and Sociology at National University of Ireland, Galway. Tereza has a long-standing research interest in the topic of mentoring phenomena and on children and young people, their lives, experiences and perspectives, and socio-ecological factors that impact on their positive development. She is especially interested in the youth mentoring relationships, role of mentors, and significant adults in positive development, and participatory research methods with children. Tereza currently works as a postdoctoral researcher at the NUI Galway in Ireland, exploring children's attitudes to science and scientists (CATSS Study, 2019–2020).

Gabriela Seidlová Málková is Associate Professor at the Charles University, Prague, the Czech Republic. She has broad research interests in literacy, language, cognitive processes related to literacy, and their development. She is intensively involved in the implementation of research outcomes into the practical fields of counselling and educational psychology in her country. Her publications include a number of assessment or intervention materials, as well as books and papers dealing with various aspects of language, literacy, cognition, and learning development.

Preface

During these first decades of the twenty-first century, there has been growing concern about increasing social inequalities in many contexts. The redistributive policies of national welfare states seem to fall short in responding to the new challenges we face and to the metamorphosis that our society is undergoing. In addition, existing political and social instability in many countries, and the rise of the far right and populism – in its various forms – make it more complex to address one of the most important challenges we have: for all children and young people to be able to realise their full potential with autonomy and a critical view of the world. Some media, state agencies, or politicians hinder this when the image they portray of certain children, young people, and their families seeking a better life in a new context is, rather, demonising and stigmatising.

During the 1980s and 1990s, mentoring for children and young people was proposed as a solution to improve their living conditions from a neoliberal perspective. The Reagan and Thatcher governments, and later others seeking a third way, called on the population as if, with cuts to the welfare state, organised citizens had a responsibility to help the poor out of poverty with a certain disinhibition of responsibility of the role of the state in this mission. From this neoliberal perspective, the mentor prototype is usually represented by a male, most often White and successful in the business world. This paternalistic view – still embedded in some programmes – aims to "save" children and young people from their context and to prevent them from eventually coming into contact with crime networks or turning down the "wrong" path. This model has been criticised lately in many contexts and there is considerable debate at the academic and social levels as to whether this is indeed the way to promote social inclusion and to support individuals and families in socially disadvantaged situations.

An example of this debate is found in the United Kingdom, where, in the late 1990s, mentoring was promoted by the Blair government to encourage the inclusion of young people who had dropped out of school. Colley (2003) critically emphasised that mentoring should not be based on an atomising approach that would focus only on a specific area (e.g. access to the labour market). Rather, she asserted that mentoring should be carried out from a more inclusive and emancipatory perspective, which respects the needs of young people and fosters community relations that go beyond the more classical one-on-one mentoring.

The last three decades have seen a considerable increase in mentoring programmes, not only in Anglo-Saxon contexts but also in others where the welfare state and redistribution policies are more significant than those in the Anglo-Saxon countries (Denmark, Sweden, or Germany, e.g.). This growth could be attributed to the mimetic effect of extrapolating neoliberal policies or logic to other political regimes that have reduced public policy investment in recent years and have increased their public debt. However, we must be cautious and rigorous and not reduce the great diversity of existing approaches only to neoliberal logic. Schwartz and Rhodes (2016) emphasise that a paradigm shift in the approach of mentoring programmes is essential to move towards a more empowering logic facilitating the development of meaningful relationships chosen by the young people themselves. In this regard, mentoring programmes need to ensure stable relationships through good pairing, but must also seek to work on a number of skills for mentees to become more self-reliant and be able to identify adults around them that can give them support at crucial moments in their life trajectories.

The debate on how to empower our children and young people through various types of support is and will be increasingly relevant in our society. This book explores different theoretical and practical perspectives and analysis on how mentoring relationships can foster empowerment processes in our youth. For example, how these relationships can foster community development and encourage access to social capital and the autonomy of the child or young person. We understand that youth empowerment can be developed through accompaniment relationships that encourage joint reflection and dialogue on how society is structured and how to contribute to improving the present world (Freire, 1997). The various chapters of this book have also been written from the desire to contribute examples of how mentoring programmes can foster these processes, so that academics as well as students and practitioners can find some examples related to practice as well.

In the first chapter, Prieto-Flores et al. highlight the role that social capital can play in mentoring relationships and the need to take this perspective into account when working with youth. Generally, the study of mentoring has been done from a psychological and developmental perspective. Although this view has been interesting and necessary, the analysis of mentoring relationships also needs to contemplate a sociological perspective that complements the previous one. In this regard, the authors emphasise the potential of mentoring programmes to promote social capital and foster formal mentoring relationships that can also promote natural mentoring relationships – that is, those that may emerge without the intervention of a programme. In the next chapter, Brady and Dolan emphasise the relevance of the concept of "presence" (Baart, 2002) to understand quality youth mentoring relationships with children and young people. The "presence approach" means that the worker or volunteer is *there for others* without focusing directly on problem solving. Presence practitioners take time to get to know the person and their environment in depth and strive to affirm the fundamental dignity of the person and establish more egalitarian relationships. For their part, Sánchez et al. point out how mentoring can promote critical consciousness among mentors, thus fostering relationships that critically reflect on their own power, privilege, and biases, and enable them to learn about systems of oppression that marginalise many of the young people served by mentoring programmes. If this condition is not met, the mentoring relationship may, however unintentionally, further alienate youth and reinforce structural inequality. In the following chapter, Schwartz et al. introduce Youth-Initiated Mentoring (YIM), in which adolescents recruit an adult from their community, with training and support provided by programme staff. The authors point out that traditional approaches to mentoring have a number of limitations and that this alternative can foster empowerment relationships. In turn, they present some examples that have been launched in the United States. Youth-Initiated Mentoring has also been implemented, concurrently, in other contexts. In this regard, Van Dam et al. show us how this perspective has been applied in the Netherlands, and examine the characteristics and phases of these programmes. In their chapter, Simoes et al. take us to Portugal to offer a holistic view of the support that children and young people receive through their mentoring relationships. The authors emphasise the need to analyse the amalgam of multiple social supports that young people have while paying particular attention to their attunement or misattunement, to finally point out the practical implications of the perspective they propose. In the last chapter, Brumovská and Seidlová emphasise the need to evaluate the quality of mentoring relationships from a qualitative point of view and from the interpretative paradigm. In recent years, the assessment of the quality of mentoring relationships from a quantitative perspective has been hegemonic; however, quite the contrary, we have realised that this is not enough. In this regard, they give examples of how various evaluations performed from this paradigm can also provide interesting insights and practical implications for youth mentoring programmes. Finally, the concluding chapter highlights the need to move towards strategies that go further in this direction of empowerment, and increase the amount of research that provides evidence on the effects that these relationships have on the well-being and social inclusion of our children and young people.

References

Colley, H. (2003). *Mentoring for social inclusion: A critical approach to nurturing mentor relationships.* London: Routledge.

Freire, P. (1997). *Mentoring the mentor. A critical dialogue with Paulo Freire.* New York: Peter Lang.

Schwartz, S.E.O. and Rhodes, J.E. (2016). From treatment to empowerment: New approaches to youth mentoring. *American Journal of Community Psychology, 58*(1–2), 150–157.

Chapter 1

Critical autonomy, social capital, and mentoring programmes for children and youth[1]

Òscar Prieto-Flores, Jordi Feu, Xavier Casademont, and Xavier Alarcón

In recent decades, the number of youth mentoring programmes has grown considerably in different countries around the world. The reasons that have favoured this increase depend on the context. In the case of Europe, for example, this increase is due to the need to provide a response to the new context of reception of immigrants and refugees, many of them unaccompanied minors or young people; while in the United States, the approach has been aimed more at reducing social inequality and preventing crime among minority youth (Preston, Prieto-Flores, & Rhodes, 2019). Regardless of the programmes' approach, their increase in recent years has led to some debates on how mentoring organisations can improve the quality of their programmes and promote, more fully, the well-being and empowerment of the children and young people they serve. In this regard, it should be pointed out that their empowerment can only be understood if they are able to develop greater critical autonomy and access to networks of social capital. Doyal and Gough (1991) defined *critical autonomy* as "the capacity to compare cultural rules, to reflect upon the rules of one's own culture, to work with others to change them and, *in extremis*, to move to another culture" (pp. 187–188), which requires the capacity for freedom of agency, political freedom, and freedom of action. And, as we know, even in the most democratic countries, such freedoms are compromised by the existence of structural forces that, explicitly or implicitly, constrain them, especially among young people from cultural minorities, migrant youth who lose their legal status as they turn 18 and become "adults", as well as young people with low incomes. With regard to social capital, there are a number of definitions that will be addressed later, but one vague and initial definition would be the possibility of attaining certain social resources through occasional or recurrent support from individuals or social institutions. For example, Ibrahim, a Moroccan boy who has just arrived to Spain and is from a working-class family where only one of the parents works and neither of them completed school, has to face many more obstacles than a child with middle-class parents who went to university. Some of the obstacles or challenges the first child faces are (a) *linguistic capital*: not just acquiring linguistic competence in the new language, but also understanding the linguistic codes associated with it; (b) *sociability and sense of belonging*: having to establish new friendships and build a new daily life with cultural challenges due to racism in the host society; (c) *cultural and social capital*: having to cope with educational and social expectations that limit his/her action, as well as difficulties in accessing support and information networks; and, finally, (d) *economic capital*: not being able to access extracurricular activities that the second child can. Mentoring can contribute to the development of critical autonomy, especially in the first three situations, but the existing literature has not taken these aspects into consideration much because until now studies on the effects of mentoring programmes with young immigrants or refugees have been scarce or very undeveloped (Oberoi, 2016).

Generally, the research that has been done on youth mentoring has been carried out in the field of psychology in the United States. It is not surprising, then, that the focus of the studies conducted thus far and the analysis of the effects of mentoring have taken into account elements of analysis characteristic of this field; for example, the effects that mentoring has on the emotional support of the child or young person, on their health and well-being, or on their academic engagement. These elements have been central in much of the research that has been done up to the present and are part of the main corpus of the most recent meta-analyses (DuBois et al., 2011; Raposa et al., 2019). Another element that has been taken into consideration is the duration of mentoring relationships and their quality, stressing that longer-lasting and quality mentoring relationships are those that tend to have greater effects on protégés (Deutsch & Spencer, 2009; Rhodes & DuBois, 2006). However, the theoretical contributions that highlight how mentoring programmes can facilitate access to networks of social capital have been very embryonic, with some exceptions (Keller & Blakeslee, 2014; Prieto-Flores & Feu, 2018; Stanton-Salazar, 2011). In this regard, more empirical studies that take this into consideration are beginning to emerge, like the work of Shier, Gouthro, and de Goias (2018), which highlights some existing interrelations between social capital and a mentoring programme with minority girls between ages 14 and 17. The authors conclude that the programme they analysed promotes access to the social capital of the protégés and enables their social networks to expand through the relationships they had with their mentors and other agents. Another example is the work of Raithelhuber (2019), who analyses the support that a mentoring programme can offer to unaccompanied refugee minors in Austria, highlighting how minors perceive the ethnic discrimination they suffer and how their mentors can provide them with emotional and psychosocial support and enhancement of their social capital. It is necessary to study this area in depth in order to observe all the different types of relations that can arise between a mentor and his protégé, and how mentoring organisations may, or may not, play an important role in promoting these.

Before proceeding, we feel it is important to differentiate between sociability and social capital because they are distinct notions that can sometimes be confused, although they may be related since by working on sociability or extraversion the protégé will have a greater possibility of connecting with support networks than without them. By sociability, we refer to the capacity to relate with and trust others, both individuals and collectives, and for extroversion. In contrast, by social capital, we refer to relationships of mutual trust and recognition between people that facilitate access to certain social environments or milieus. For example, in the case of Ibrahim, improving his Spanish thanks to the relationship with his mentor made it easier for him to socialise more with other pupils at his school. Another element that helped was his continuous talks with his mentor about his being accepted or not by the rest of his classmates. These can help to relativise some erroneous perceptions (e.g. thinking that his classmates don't like or accept him when that is not the case) or give situations of concern the importance they deserve (e.g. bullying and racist attitudes). But that does not mean that, thanks to this opening, the protégé accesses networks of social and cultural capital beyond the relationship with his mentor.

With the aim of contributing to this area, this chapter focuses on clarifying how the concept of social capital is used in the mentoring literature, and on improving the understanding of mentoring relationships from a broad vision that fosters the empowerment of children and young people. The concept of social capital is one of the most frequently used sociological concepts in recent years, not only from sociology but from other social sciences disciplines as well. From our point of view, it is a concept that, at times, has been used vaguely and can thus generate confusion. This conceptual clarification, which we will undertake in this chapter, may not only provide researchers with a more precise definition of the concept in the field of mentoring in general, but also enable mentoring programme staff to take social capital into account in their programmes to promote the empowerment of children and young people. In order to understand and examine it properly, we propose, finally, an interpretative frame that takes into consideration the different levels at which access to social capital can be promoted, or not, related to critical autonomy in children and young people.

Definition of social capital and its relationships with mentoring

Two eminent sociologists like Pierre Bourdieu in Europe and James S. Coleman in the United States defined social capital in similar ways in the early 1980s. For Bourdieu, while economic capital can be transformed into money or be institutionalised into property rights, and cultural capital into academic credentials, social capital "is the aggregate of the actual or potential resources which are linked to the possession of a durable network of more or less institutionalised relationships of mutual acquaintance and recognition" (1980, p. 2). The amount of social capital that an individual possesses depends, then, on the amount of network connections available. For Coleman (1988), social capital "is defined by its function. It is not a single entity but a variety of different entities, with two elements in common: they all consist of some aspect of social structures, and they facilitate certain actions of actors – whether persons or corporate actors- within the structure. Like other forms of capital, social capital is productive, making possible the achievement of certain ends that in its absence would not be possible" (p. S98). Both authors' definitions are similar, although Coleman's definition is more optimistic than Bourdieu's and only considers social capital as facilitating "positive" resources like school success. It does not contemplate the possibility that young people can access networks of "negative" social capital that promote access to deviant behaviour and processes of social exclusion, like belonging to certain youth gangs (Portes, 1998).

As well as taking into account the strong social bonds that some people or groups might have, Mark Granovetter (1973) also highlights the potential that weak bonds have for facilitating access to certain jobs. In this regard, it is interesting to observe not only how people can have a close relationship with their ethnic group or relatives and thanks to this can obtain work, but also how weak bonds can also have a similar effect on these people's access to the labour market. Later, the political scientist Robert Putnam (1995) draws on Granovetter's notion of weak bonds to differentiate two types of social capital, what he calls *bonding social capital* and *bridging social capital*. While the first are usually strong bonds that occur between members of the same social group or homogenous groups and can serve as social closure or intragroup solidarity, the second can play the role of bridging different networks and "can generate broader identities and reciprocity" (p. 23). In this regard, mentoring programmes designed to promote intercultural relations between young immigrants and university students can have the characteristics of bridging social capital because they create relationships between people from different networks who would otherwise not have met. But Putnam's conceptualisation of social capital possesses a number of ambiguities that need to be clarified since, as Ricardo Stanton-Salazar (personal communication, November 15, 2019) highlights, "for the sake of precise theory development, it is important to differentiate Putnam's Social Capital as either (a) network structure that leads to advantages, or (b) potential benefits that can potentially spring forth from network or tie structure" (p. 5). In this regard, it should be pointed out that one thing is to facilitate connection with someone from a network different to one's own (through a mentor), and another quite different thing is whether this connection brings benefits or not for those involved, especially the mentee. This last point is only slightly or not at all developed in Putnam's theory, but it is of great importance when it comes to understanding how such relationships can facilitate access to institutional agents or real resources.

Ricardo Stanton-Salazar (2011) also highlights the existence of an *empowerment social capital* "characterized by the provision of institutional support by critically conscious institutional agents, and comes with a socialization agenda aimed at transforming the consciousness of those they support, and at encouraging them to also become moral and caring agents to changing the world" (p. 1090). He highlights that these relationships can facilitate inclusion processes of low-income Latino youth in the United States but, to do so, the mentors would need to teach counter-stratification strategies and critical consciousness to the mentees. In line with this thought-provoking work, mentoring programmes could include strategies and processes that not only serve to promote social and educational inclusion but also to encourage the development of critical thinking and the role of a mentor who fosters the development of the mentee based on their interests and motivations. In the words of Paulo Freire (1997), when asked if one can be a mentor/guide without being an oppressor: "what I mean is that to be an authentic mentor, the teacher (or the person) should not adopt the role of mentor [...] The authentic practice of the mentor resides in the fact that the mentor refuses to take control of the life, dreams, and aspirations of the mentee. Because by not doing so we could very easily fall into a type of paternalistic mentorship (p. 324)".

In this regard, we understand the role that Stanton-Salazar and Freire attribute to the mentor as someone who has the ability to identify what social inequalities condition the freedom of the mentee, what motivations and interests the child and adolescent have, and how through both dialogue and action they can build (also in collaboration with others) a scaffolding that facilitates their development and autonomy – all of this without an attitude of wanting to impose their vision onto the mentee in a paternalistic way. This is no easy task, and those who act as mentors need to have proper training and also internalise the above skills in order to be able to transmit them to others.

As well as clearly identifying how mentors, at an individual level, can facilitate access to social capital, it is necessary to take into account the role that mentoring organisations can play in promoting such a task. That is to say, how the organisations can facilitate, or not, the development of networks of social capital and of critical consciousness. In this regard, the sociologist Mario L. Small (2009), for example, highlights how organisations, not just individuals, can "effectively brokering social capital", be it purposely or not purposely. For Small, organisations can promote norms and generate roles that help to "connect an individual to another individual, to another organization, or to the resources they contain" (p. 19). As an example, he studies the case of childcare centres in New York and how these institutions can facilitate the generation of social bonds that promote networks of social capital and well-being of the mothers that normally take part in the everyday life of these centres. Along similar lines, mentoring programmes can also carry out this mission of connecting two (or more) people in a regular and cooperative manner with a clear purpose through an informal relationship. What is needed is to delve deeper into how these relations can have a richer and deeper impact on the empowerment of the children and youth involved.

Shift towards empowerment approaches to mentoring

In recent years, some psychologists have proposed innovation in the field of youth mentoring by emphasising the limitations of traditional treatment approaches based solely on one-to-one mentoring (Liang, Spencer, West, & Rappaport, 2013; Rhodes & Schwartz, 2016). Instead of directing all the resources to generate a link only with the mentor chosen by the mentoring organisation, other informal support is encouraged with *caring* adults who are accessible to them in their natural networks. From this viewpoint, it is important that children and young people learn to develop skills so they can build their own informal support networks and not depend solely on their mentor (by "putting all the eggs in the same basket", so to speak). Some programmes that employ this approach are called *Youth-Initiated Mentoring*, in which young people "nominate adults to serve as their mentors, selecting from among the adults who are already in their social networks" (p. 154). Another programme, described in this book, that operates along similar lines is *Connected Scholars*, which provides support to high school and university students to help them develop their own support networks (Schwartz et al., 2016).

It should also be noted that the scientific literature has emphasised that the generation of a strong tie is required for a mentoring relationship to work and to be of quality. However, there are an increasing number of studies that highlight the need to go beyond whether this tie between mentor and mentee is a lasting or strong one in order to fulfil the specific programme objectives efficiently. Cavell and Elledge (2013) pointed out that mentoring is an efficient but underdeveloped tool and that we need to examine the nature of the best practices that can be generated within the mentoring relationship based on the stated objectives. This debate leads us to ask ourselves how we can generate mentoring relationships that help the people we serve more and better, and how each programme identifies and foments the most effective practices that empower children and young people. In this regard, Jean E. Rhodes (2018) recently highlighted the need to create *recursive dynamics*, meaning a series of practices that the mentor promotes such that the more they are carried out in their day-to-day relationship, the more they are internalised by the mentee and help to consolidate learnings that facilitate his/her social inclusion. These learnings and scaffolding remain in the mentee once the mentor is no longer there or when the programme or mentoring relationship has concluded. For example, the mentee can develop a series of skills to establish new relationships with adults around him that can help him and potentially become his/her informal mentors. Going back to the case of Ibrahim, in the conversations that he has with his mentor, he realises that he also can count on some secondary school teachers for emotional support. Knowing how to identify them and approaching them was crucial for Ibrahim to gain support from several teachers and for one of them to become an institutional agent helping him to prepare for the university entrance examination.

From our perspective, this paradigm change towards a perspective of empowerment not only promotes the creation of new programmes that have this holistic vision, but they also challenge the traditional mentoring programmes to go beyond one-to-one mentoring by placing the relationship between the child or young person and their mentor in a context of broader interpersonal relationships (of social networks). There have so far been few studies that examine deeply the relations between social capital, critical autonomy (or empowerment), and mentoring programmes. It is, therefore, necessary to examine, both conceptually and practically, how mentoring programmes take into account social networks, existing power relations in society, and social capital to facilitate greater empowerment of children and young people.

The multi-level social capital framework for mentoring programmes

In addition to the effect that mentoring relationships may have on the development of the child and young person, a comprehensive approach to mentoring relationships should also take into account the different levels of power relations that exist between mentor and protégé, the relevance of social capital and the potential that children and young people have to access – or not – certain social relationships. In this framework, four interconnected dimensions (two at the *micro*-level, one at the *meso*-level and another at the *macro*-level) can be observed that are important to understanding the connections between mentoring, social capital, and the empowerment of children and young people (protégés) – see Table 1.1.

Table 1.1 The multilevel social capital framework for mentoring programmes

		Role	Function	Programme staff recommendations
Micro-level	Mentor	Institutional agent	Provide one's own resources	i, ii, iii
		Bridging agent or actor-driven brokerage	Facilitate access either to resources embedded in mentors' egocentric network or from mentee's natural network	iv
Meso-level	Mentoring organisations	Institutional brokers of social capital		v, vi
Macro-level	Other social and political actors	Builders/creators of mentoring programmes engagement	Promote political orientations towards more inclusive mentoring perspectives that facilitate a vision of fomenting critical autonomy and social capital	vii, viii

The micro-level of the mentor as institutional agent

Sometimes when we refer to social capital, we do so in relation to how the mentor can facilitate the mentee's access to new networks and contacts. But it is also important to observe how the mentor can facilitate access to certain resources for the mentee that, in the absence of such a relationship, would not have occurred. For example, when the mentor can be of great help to clarify doubts the mentee may have regarding the understanding of school material, when they visit the university and they speak about the previous experience of the mentor and the future of the mentee, and when the mentor shows him/her how to navigate the educational system to access higher education through different itineraries. In this regard, the mentor can be considered an *institutional agent*, "an individual who occupies one or more hierarchical positions of relatively high-status and authority [...] situated in an adolescent's social network" (Stanton-Salazar, 2011, p. 1067). While it is true that some mentoring programmes try to ensure that the mentee is from the same milieu as the adolescent or young mentee (*Youth-Initiated Mentoring*), most of them usually connect with people they do not previously know and that come from different social backgrounds. In both cases, if the mentor that acts as an institutional agent comes from a different social class and/or ethnic origin than the mentee, it is likely that different lifestyles or *habitus* conditioned by the generation of "thoughts, perceptions, expressions, and actions – whose limits are set by the historically and socially situated conditions of its production" (Bourdieu, 1990, p. 55) will become evident in their meetings and conversations. Such differences can condition the relationship and the mentor needs to have a critical consciousness, know how to initiate meaningful conversations with his/her mentee, and interpret together the social inequalities and the possibilities of reflection and action of a practice that is transformative or connected to social change. Some years ago, Liang et al. (2013) highlighted the need for mentoring programmes to promote mentor–mentee relationships that are less hierarchical and more egalitarian that give prominence and voice to the adolescents, in which there is mutual learning and where the existing social barriers are critically addressed.

There are certain external elements that need to be considered for the mentor to have an impact and the mentoring relationship to be successful. For example, Keller and Blakeslee (2014) stressed the importance of counting on the family or tutors of the protégé in order to foster trust towards the mentor and his/her milieu and thus consolidate the relationship. Without such a climate of trust, it is unlikely that a meaningful mentor–mentee relationship can be built. Another potentially significant factor in the relations between social capital, critical autonomy, and mentoring is whether or not the mentor's cultural and social background is the same as the mentee's (Crul & Akdeniz, 1997). If it is, the mentoring could be more culturally significant because the mentor knows the cultural and symbolic codes of the protégé's daily life well and can help him/her navigate between two symbolically different worlds that can clash and be contradictory. However, until now there has been no empirical evidence supporting such relationships of similar ethnic background over other cross-cultural ones.

Some recommendations for the programme staff are as follows:

i Help to establish an enduring, trusting, and quality relationship.
ii Make sure parents or tutors actively support the relationship.
iii Train the mentors and give them support, if they need it, so that they can play the role of gatekeepers in the access to certain resources, information, and internalisation of practices.

The micro-level of the mentor as a bridging agent between mentor and protégé networks (how the mentor can act as a bridging agent through his/her egocentric network or even through the mentee natural network)

This type of relationship can be conceptualised as *actor-driven brokerage* because it is the mentor, as an individual, who makes these connections in intentional or unintentional ways. One example could be when Ibrahim's mentor introduced him to Javier, an aerospace engineer, because Ibrahim was interested in aeronautics and space stations. Ibrahim would probably not have begun a relationship with this engineer through his personal network (*mentor egocentric network*). The mentor could also discuss with Ibrahim which of his teachers might support him in his interests and motivations (*mentee network*). Here it is important to stress that not all connections, be they of the mentor or mentee, can be considered, in themselves, social capital ones. Only those that can facilitate access to resources would not have occurred without them. Let us imagine that Ibrahim established a tie with one of his teachers who then became an institutional agent and helped Ibrahim have access to an educational track or stream focused on studying engineering. This situation took place in this case and the mentoring experience had a ripple effect on his educational trajectory.

Some recommendations for programme staff:

iv Select mentors who have extended networks and/or know how to help to navigate through resources, especially those connected with the aim of the programme.

The meso-level of mentoring organisations (how mentoring programmes explicitly take into account social capital and relationships of social inequality)

Some authors, like Smith (2008), have pointed out that some mentoring programmes can create "social capital and link students to schools with better resources and, critically, with stronger links to college" (p. 287). However, how such relationships are created in the framework of mentoring projects is, at present, a gap in our knowledge that needs to be explored more deeply. Nevertheless, it should be pointed out that beyond the individual action of the mentor, it is important to identify how mentoring organisations can become institutional brokers of social capital. According to Small (2009), this takes place when an organisation effectively connects an individual to another individual, or to another organisation. In this regard, we consider that mentoring organisations can take into account, explicitly, the promotion of relationships of social capital, critical consciousness, and the promotion of critical autonomy. An example of this is how *Youth-Initiated Mentoring* programmes actively enable the mentee to choose his/her mentor from agents in his network. Another example is that of those mentoring organisations that generate training materials and socialise their mentors, meaning the internalisation of guidelines and norms and that orient their actions.

Some recommendations for programme staff are as follows:

v Select mentors with prior experience of working with children and youth if possible.
vi Train and support mentors in how to teach children and young people to reach other adults from mentor egocentric networks or from their own network connected to their interests.
vii Train and support mentors in how to cultivate critical consciousness in their mentees by establishing a non-paternalistic relationship.

Finally, *the* macro-level of the sociopolitical context where mentoring is carried out

It is important to highlight that the predominant ideological approach underlying mentoring programmes depends on various social and political actors. Governments or other funders may condition the political agenda and approach of the programmes. This happens especially when organisations working at street-level may adjust programme goals to be congruent with policy intent (Garrow & Grusky, 2012). In recent years, some state agencies have launched campaigns and have dedicated funds to promote mentoring programmes with a particular perspective and with apparent neutrality. An example of this situation is critically outlined by Helen Colley (2003) in the United Kingdom, when she analyses the increase in mentoring programmes for social inclusion during the time of Tony Blair and the "third way" at the end of the 1990s. The Labour government greatly increased support for mentoring (*engagement mentoring*) focused on the labour market inclusion of disaffected youth. Far from a perspective of empowerment, this approach promoted the acquisition of a *habitus* of behaviour and low job expectations that entered into contradiction, in some cases, with the personal agenda of the protégés. Colley observed how the focus of the programme generated conflicts and power relationships between mentors (university students) and the disaffected young people, as some mentors were sensitive to the young person's personal agenda that diverged from the orientation of the programme "of low expectations", while other mentors only adhered to the marked agenda. Another more recent example in the same context was the campaign that Prime Minister David Cameron launched in 2016 with the name "Life Chances Strategy", a campaign in which some mentoring programmes improved the opportunities of the "poor" youngsters, thanks to the participation of "high-quality mentors" and inspirational business men and women that act as "role models to help young people make big plans for their future" (United Kingdom Government, 2016). However, hegemonic narratives about approaches to child and youth mentoring may offer different perspectives than the neoliberal one from Blair and Cameron's governments. In this regard, the growing number of federations of mentoring programmes can advocate to promote political orientations towards more inclusive perspectives that facilitate the critical autonomy and social capital of the children and young people they serve, as we have highlighted in this chapter. In this way, the programmes can boast a more positive and empowering approach rather than a deficit-based and paternalistic one. Some of these organisations that can play this role are *MENTOR, the National Mentoring Partnership* (1990) in the United States, the *Scottish Mentoring Network* (1997), the *New Zealand Youth Mentoring Network* (2001), la *Coordinadora de Mentoría Social* (2012) in Spain, and the *Canadian Mentoring Partnership* (2016). To do this, these federations need to be able to generate training material and gather knowledge, together with universities, on what mentoring practices can lead to greater critical autonomy and greater access to the social capital of children and young people. Finally, it should be pointed out that this advocacy work can also be done, hand in hand, with international organisations that advise governments like UNESCO, the European Commission, OECD, UNICEF, and the World Bank.

Some recommendations to mentoring federations and policy makers are as follows:

viii Create material, together with researchers, on what mentoring practices promote greater access to social capital and greater critical autonomy.
ix Do work with policymakers from national and international organisations on how to facilitate policies that take into account a more emancipatory conception of mentoring programmes.

Conclusion

In recent years, the need to search for new paradigms of social intervention that examine more deeply the social inclusion of children and young people has become evident. In the specific field of mentoring, this has focused on how processes of adolescent emancipation can be facilitated in order to establish caring relationships with agents from their own social networks, or with other people that belong to other social networks, and thus open new doors that, without them, would not have been possible. As previously noted, in order to act with greater precision we need to understand how these relationships facilitate access to networks of social capital at different levels: that the mentor acts as an institutional or empowering agent; that she/he facilitates bonds with other agents of the same network as the mentee or of his/her own network; that the mentoring programmes guide his/her training and the support of the mentors and mentees towards social capital and critical autonomy, and so forth. And in this regard, mentoring programmes play a very important role since they can work in association with other organisations to advocate for and foment this debate and change of paradigm, in both national and transnational political contexts.

With this paradigm change in mind, it is necessary to begin providing these approaches content, making promising experiences visible and evaluating their impact through both quantitative and qualitative research. Furthermore, it would also be interesting to create a common database with recursive dynamics that mentors can use to promote these processes of empowerment and help to facilitate content to the structure of these programmes.

In general, studies that have analysed the impact of mentoring programmes have been experimental or quasi-experimental, normally observing their short-term impact (between 6 and 15 months). There are very few longitudinal studies that have analysed the impact of mentoring over several years and none, as far as we can see, has observed what happens with the mentoring relationships that continue and those that do not, once the programmes have formally concluded. One hypothesis would be that, if some continue and their mentors continue playing this social capital and support role, the impact would be greater and more evident. For example, two years after concluding his mentoring, Ibrahim went with his mentor to a university fair. His mentor went from being a formally constituted mentor to a natural one, having informal meetings at the weekends or when they met in their neighbourhood. Another hypothesis is that this type of relationship can happen more frequently in certain cultural contexts (e.g. rural and peri-urban ones), where they can become more consolidated than in others. Properly understanding the mechanisms involved how and why such continuations occur is very interesting and has practical implications for helping to bridge the *mentoring gap* between middle-class and low-income families shown in previous sociological and political science scholarship (Erikson, McDonald, & Elder, 2009; Putnam, 2015).

All this does not mean that mentoring programmes, which entail a qualitative leap over traditional volunteering, might denaturalise. Today, the risk of generalising mentoring programmes based on fashionable policies and the routinisation of public policies can be significant and could harm not only the children and young people but also the volunteers that participate. To avoid this, the approach, methodology, and monitoring of these programmes need to be crafted with rigour and quality.

This journey has just begun and we hope that in the coming years there will be more evidence available that can provide relevant information for new programmes or change the approach of some existing ones. For this, social scientists from different disciplines need to work together, side by side, with mentoring programme professionals and with methodological perspectives that enable the voice of the children and young people that we serve to emerge.

As Constantine Cavafy writes in his poem Ithaka, "hope your road is a long one, full of adventure, full of discovery".

Note

1. This chapter was written in dialogue between Òscar Prieto-Flores and Dr. Ricardo Stanton-Salazar. The first author is grateful for his guide, commitment, and the time he gave to discuss this important topic.

References

Bourdieu, P. (1980). Le Capital Social. Notes Provisoires. *Actes de la Recherche en Sciences Sociales, 31*, 2–3.
Bourdieu, P. (1990). *The logic of practice*. Stanford, CA: Stanford University Press.
Cavell, T. A., & Elledge, L. C. (2013). Mentoring and prevention science. In D. DuBois, & M. J. Karcher (Eds.), *Handbook of youth mentoring* (pp. 29–42). New York, NY: SAGE.

Coleman, J. S. (1988). Social capital in the creation of human capital. *The American Journal of Sociology, 94,* S95–S120.

Colley, H. (2003). *Mentoring for social inclusion: A critical approach to nurturing mentor relationships.* London: Routledge.

Crul, M., & Akdemiz, A. (1997). *Het huiswerkbegeleidingsproject van SOEBA.* Amsterdam: SOEBA.

Deutsch, N. L., & Spencer, R. (2009). Capturing the magic: Assessing the quality of youth mentoring relationships. *New Directions for Youth Development, 121,* 47–70.

Doyal, L., & Gough, I. (1991). *A theory of human need.* London: Macmillan.

DuBois, D. L., Portillo, N., Rhodes, J. E., Silverthorn, N., & Valentine, J. C. (2011). How effective are mentoring programs for youth? A systematic assessment of the evidence. *Psychological Science in the Public Interest, 12*(2), 57–91.

Erikson, L. D., McDonald, S., & Elder, G. H. Jr. (2009). Informal mentors and education: Complementary or compensatory resources? *Sociology of Education, 82*(4), 344–367.

Freire, P. (1997). *Mentoring the mentor. A critical dialogue with Paulo Freire.* New York, NY: Peter Lang. https://www.youtube.com/watch?v=Jz68ibK1Mno

Garrow, E. E., & Grusky, O. (2012). Institutional logic and street-level discretion: The case of HIV test counseling. *Journal of Public Administration Research and Theory, 23,* 103–131.

Granovetter, M. (1973). The strength and the weak ties. *The American Journal of Sociology, 78*(6), 1360–1380.

Keller, T. E., & Blakeslee, J. E. (2014). Social networks and mentoring. In D. DuBois, & M. J. Karcher (Eds.), *Handbook of youth mentoring* (pp. 129–142). New York, NY: SAGE.

Liang, B., Spencer, R., West, J., & Rappaport, N. (2013). Expanding the reach of youth mentoring: Partnering with youth for personal growth and social change. *Journal of Adolescence, 36,* 257–267.

Oberoi, A. K. (2016). *Mentoring for First-Generation Immigrant and Refugee Youth.* National Mentoring Resource Center Population Review. Retrieved from http://www.nationalmentoringresourcecenter.org

Portes, A. (1998). Social capital: Its origins and applications in modern sociology. *Annual Review of Sociology, 24,* 1–24.

Preston, J. M., Prieto-Flores, Ò., & Rhodes, J. E. (2019). Mentoring in context: A comparative study of youth mentoring programs in the United States and Continental Europe. *Youth & Society, 57*(7), 900–914.

Prieto-Flores, Ò., & Feu, J. (2018). What type of impact could social mentoring programs have? An exploration of the existing assessments and a proposal of an analytical framework. *Pedagogía Social: Revista Interuniversitaria, 31,* 149–162.

Putnam, R. D. (1995). *Bowling alone: America's declining social capital.* New York, NY: Simon & Schuster.

Putnam, R. D. (2015). *Our kids: The American dream in crisis.* New York, NY: Simon & Schuster.

Raithelhuber, E. (2019). "If we want, they help us in any way": how unaccompanied refugee minors' experience mentoring relationships. *European Journal of Social Work,* 1–16. https://doi.org/10.1080/13691457.2019.1606787

Raposa, E. B., Rhodes, J. E., Stams, G. J. J. M., Card, N., Burton, S., Schwartz, S., Yoviene Sykes, L. A., Kanchewa, S., Kupersmidt, J., … Hussain, S. (2019). The effects of youth mentoring programs: A meta-analysis of outcome studies. *Journal of Youth and Adolescence, 48*(3), 423–443.

Rhodes, J. E. (2018). *Research on quality of mentoring relationships: How to build strong relationships.* Retrieved from https://mentoringsummit.eu/speakers/jean-rhodes]

Rhodes, J. E., & DuBois, D. L. (2006). Understanding and facilitating the youth mentoring movement. *Social Policy Report of the Society for Research in Child Development, XX*(III), 3–19.

Schwartz, S. E. O., Kanchewa, S. S., Rhodes, J. E., Cutler, E., & Cunningham, J. L. (2016). I didn't know you could just ask: Empowering underrepresented college-bound students to recruit academic and career mentors. *Children and Youth Services Review, 64*, 51–59.

Shier, M. L., Gouthro, S., & de Goias, R. (2018). The pursuit of social capital among adolescent high school aged girls: The role of formal mentor-mentee relationships. *Children and Youth Services Review, 93*, 276–282.

Small, M. L. (2009). *Unanticipated gains. Origins of network inequality in everyday life.* New York, NY: Oxford University Press.

Smith, R. C. (2008). Horatio Alger lives in Brooklyn: Extrafamily support, intrafamily dynamics, and socially neutral operating identities in exceptional mobility among children of Mexican immigrants. *The Annals of the American Academy of Political and Social Science, 620*, 270–290.

Stanton-Salazar, R. D. (2011). A social capital framework for the study of institutional agents and their role in the empowerment of low-status students and youth. *Youth & Society, 43*(3), 1066–1109.

United Kingdom Government. (2016). *Prime Minister's speech on life chances.* Retrieved from https://www.gov.uk/government/speeches/prime-ministers-speech-on-life-chances

Chapter 2

The importance of being present
Mentors as "presence practitioners"

Bernadine Brady and Pat Dolan

The term "youth mentoring" refers to relationships between young people and non-parental adults from whom the young person receives support and guidance (Horn & Spencer, 2018, p. 183). These relationships can occur naturally within the young person's social network or they may be facilitated by a youth mentoring programme. Research has shown that many young people derive value from these informal social connections, with evidence of better outcomes in a range of areas, including social, emotional, behavioural, and academic domains (Spencer, 2012; Van Dam et al., 2018).

Quality relationships are at the heart of the youth mentoring process. It is widely accepted that the success of youth mentoring relationships is contingent upon the development of a "strong interpersonal connection" between the mentor and the mentee (Rhodes, 2005, p. 31). Young people tend to have better outcomes where they perceive that their mentor shares similar interests, is authentic, trustworthy, honest, shows empathy, and is "there for me" (DeWit et al., 2016; Gettings & Wilson, 2014; Silke, Brady, & Dolan, 2019a).

In this chapter, we aim to reflect further on the principles associated with quality youth mentoring relationships by introducing a theoretical perspective from nursing and pastoral care, namely the "presence approach" developed by Andries Baart. The presence approach draws attention to the quality of attentiveness, listening, understanding as well as being open to the needs, wishes, requests, reasoning, and frame of reference of the care receiver that one is trying to help (Baart & Vosman, 2011; Kuis, Goossensen, Van Dijke, & Baart, 2015, p. 174). To date, the approach has been deployed primarily with regard to pastoral care and nursing, but we argue that good quality youth mentoring can be understood as an illustration of the "presence approach" in practice. In this chapter, we first introduce the concept of "presence" and outline its key principles. Second, we make a case for why it is useful to consider the "presence approach" in relation to youth mentoring. Third, we present a series of case vignettes, drawing on the narratives of three young people (from a sample of 13) who took part in a qualitative study regarding young people's experiences of youth mentoring. We then reflect on how principles associated with the presence approach are evident in the young people's stories of their mentoring experiences.

Understanding the concept of "presence"

In any human relationship, it can be strongly argued that having a sense of presence from another person in terms of their undivided and focused attention to the other person is not just desirable but fundamental. Andries Baart (2002) developed "the presence approach" arising from research on the work of neighbourhood pastoral ministers working in disadvantaged neighbourhoods in the Netherlands. In his "Introductory Sketch of the Practice", he describes the conventional practice of many health and social care professionals as an "intervention approach", involving "processes of screening and intake and which apply select remedies to specific problems". However, Baart (2002, p. 5) argues that, while "often such parceling out and fragmentation are necessary", they are at odds with "the way life is lived, particularly traumatic and chaotic lives". The personal and relational aspect of care, including compassion, caring, and comfort are being overlooked due to "a dominant focus on pathways, tasks and documentation" (Kuis et al., 2015, p. 173). Baart presents what he calls, a different way of handling social problems, which he calls "the presence approach".

A practitioner adopting a "presence approach" is a worker or volunteer who is "there for others" without focusing directly on problem-solving; "a trusted and familiar figure who knows how to listen attentively" (Baart, 2002, p. 5). Presence practitioners take time to get to know the person and their environment deeply and strive to affirm the fundamental dignity of the person. They don't meet in an office or clinic but in the course of their everyday activities. Presence practitioners don't intervene or provide solutions; according to Baart "the most important thing these pastoral ministers bring is the faithful offering of themselves" (p. 1). They are those that have time, take time, and are as he terms "free" in that they don't have alternative plans for their role or other intentions. They focus on earning trust, keeping connected, and supporting the person in personal reflection and decision-making. While not being problem-focused, these approaches may lead to problem-solving. From this orientation over time they are in a strong position to build trust with the other person, share their own history and learn from them.

Kuis et al. (2015) note that while there are many definitions of "presence" in the literature, Baart's Theory of Presence is distinguished by its inclusion of "being there for" in addition to "being there" and "being with". "Being there for", they argue involves an understanding from within a particular relationship, where it becomes clearer "what fits into the specific life of the other and what the others needs or pains are" (p. 174). It implies being there for the person beyond and "not abandoning the other emotionally or relationally" even "if no cure is available" (p. 174).

Baart (2002) developed eight key principles for presence, which were used by Kuis et al. (2015, p. 177) to inform their development of a self-evaluation tool for practitioners in nursing but with applicability for other professionals. The eight principles are described as follows:

1 **To be free for** – Rather than having their own fixed agenda, presence practitioners respond to what the other brings up.
2 **Open for** – Presence practitioners "let their armour down", thereby offering the possibility for others effectively to genuinely enter into their presence.
3 **Attentive relation** – Presence practitioners pay attention to what the other may need from them and respond with an open mind.
4 **Connecting to what exists** – Presence practitioners accept and connect to the life of the other and "do not diminish, expropriate, or overrule" in any way.
5 **Changing perspective** – Presence practitioners understand the world from the perspective of the other, including what is important and why.
6 **Being available** – Presence practitioners make their presence, skills, abilities, etc., available to the other to be deployed as needed.
7 **Patience and time** – Presence practitioners give the other ample time and space and are not rushed.
8 **Loyal dedication** – Presence practitioners are loyal and don't refuse to help even though they know that they may be taken advantage of.

Why is the presence approach relevant to youth mentoring?

We believe that the presence approach is a useful concept because it foregrounds the importance of quality relationships. In health and social care more broadly, service users' emphasis on the importance and quality of their relationship with those professionals who work with and for them has been affirmed strongly in research (Ryan, Ford, Beadsmore, & Muijen, 1999; Sudbery, 2002). For example, in a study with social work service users in palliative care services, respondents said that one of the things that they found most helpful about the social worker was the relationship that they had with them (Beresford, Croft, & Adshead, 2007). The key factors in the relationship and qualities on the part of the social worker that were welcomed by service users were consistent with the presence approach. These included a capacity to demonstrate warmth like a genuine friend, being an engaged listener, and allowing the service user to determine their own agenda. The length of time the social worker worked with them could be long or short, but the presence of the social worker including their genuine interest in them and their capacity to focus in real time while with their service user was seen as the key issue.

However, it can be argued that, in the social care field more generally, the relationship building aspect of practice has been undermined and weakened to some extent, as a consequence of neoliberal policies which have led to increased marketization of services, reduced budgets, and new forms of managerialism (Hyslop, 2018). Concerns have been expressed that there is an increasing trend for social work performance within statutory services to be reduced to a time-limited, check-box exercise, in which the relationship between social worker and service user is very much a secondary consideration (Bilson, Featherstone, & Martin, 2017; Munro, 2011). Beresford et al. (2007, p. 1388) argued that there is an obvious tension between the characteristics of practice valued by service users and "the direction of travel of social work influenced by policy and professional considerations". These concerns have led to a renewed focus on the importance of relationships in child and youth welfare practice in recent years, with calls for a move away from the dichotomy of expert–service user relationship towards more collaborative forms of practice (Golightley & Holloway, 2018; McGregor, 2019).

These issues pertaining to social work and social care more broadly are also pertinent in the context of youth mentoring programmes. It is widely accepted in the youth mentoring literature that the relationship between the mentor and mentee is the most important aspect of the intervention (Rhodes, 2005). According to Rhodes (2005), "positive outcomes only become possible if a meaningful relationship develops between the mentor and mentee, one that is characterized by mutuality, trust and empathy" (p. 31). Given the primacy of the relationship, it could be assumed that the existence of presence in a mentoring relationship can be taken for granted and should not need to be raised as an issue. However, this aspect of the mentor–mentee relationship cannot be assumed as ever present in the relationship and can be marred by over-intervention, whereby the mentor does not listen and prefers to rush in with a diagnosis and set of solutions. In other words, the relationship may be focused on what the mentor wants the youth to be and achieve, rather than being present with them to understand and connect on their level (Silke, Brady, & Dolan, 2019b).

Furthermore, it is important to reflect on the role and purpose of youth mentoring relationships in the lives of young people at risk (Prieto-Flores & Feu, 2018). Vulnerable young people taking part in youth mentoring programmes often have a range of formal professional services such as psychologists, social work, and youth justice practitioners involved in their lives. In these contexts, young people can sometimes feel powerless because many decisions made are outside of their control (Jackson, Brady, Forkan, Tierney, & Kennan, 2018) and also that they are constantly under watch (Stein, 2012). Research has found that that young people view their mentors as providing a different type of support to such professionals and different to family and friends (Brady, Dolan, & Canavan, 2017). For example, young people in care taking part in research by Brady, Dolan, and McGregor (2020) saw their mentors as someone who was "outside" of the world of systems and professionals and with whom they could be themselves. They described their mentors as easy-going, relaxed, non-judgemental, and authentic. The research participants saw clear differences between mentors and social workers, highlighting that mentors, in contrast to social workers, "don't write things down" and are "there for you" when you need them (p. 127). Many of the research participants viewed the support of their mentor as helping them to cope and thrive in their various social contexts, including home, school, and with peers. Brady et al. (2020) argue that mentors are seen by young people as part of the "life world" which refers to the lived realm of informal, culturally grounded interactions in contrast to professionals such as teachers and social workers, who are seen to represent the "system world", which is composed of formal organisations, such as governments, private companies, unions, and courts (Habermas, 2015). We argue that conceptualising youth mentoring in terms of "a presence approach" can help to safeguard the role of mentoring as an informal, non-directive, and supportive space.

As with the broader field of health and social care as discussed above, the importance of presence in mentoring relationships can be endangered by a fixation on direct positive outcomes and key performance indicators accruing from the match in order to justify continued support from their funders. For example, Helen Colley's UK study of "engagement mentoring" (2003, p. 18) for young people at risk of disengaging from or already disengaged from formal schemes of education, training, or employment found that a focus on hard outcomes in these schemes undermined the gains that were made in the areas of confidence, outlook, and aspirations. When young people were allowed to negotiate mentoring relationships on the basis of their own needs and concerns, they usually perceived mentoring in a highly positive way and could identify important benefits from the process (p. 162). Colley argues that mentors are capable of achieving private goals and ironically, if left alone to do this, these gains will aggregate into public goals but that the control exercised by formal mentoring programmes often does not allow this. Similarly, Philip and Spratt (2007) describe how the ability of the Connexions service to meet the needs of its vulnerable target group was undermined by favouring "employability" over the meeting of other needs that were important to the young people, such as housing or relationships. Overall, the research suggests that the element of coercion involved in these schemes and the prioritisation of official outcomes over the individual needs of the mentees were harmful to efforts on the parts of young people and mentors to develop trusting relationships and undermined potential gains (Colley, 2003; Meier, 2008; Philip & Spratt, 2007).

Given the increased focus on children's rights and participation in decision-making in recent years, it is important to pay attention to youth perspectives on mentoring and the characteristics they welcome in mentors. We believe that the presence approach encapsulates what young people find valuable about mentoring relationships. Research has found that young people value mentors who are easy-going, relaxed, trustworthy, and kind (Ahrens et al., 2011;

Brady et al., 2020; Munson, Smalling, Spencer, Scott, & Tracy, 2010). They also favour mentors who are "real" or authentic with them, listen to them, are not judgemental or condescending, and create spaces in which the young people feel they can talk honestly. It is important to young people that their mentors give freely of their time and truly understand them and the context within which they live their lives.

Reflecting on the presence approach in youth mentoring

We now move on to reflect more specifically on how the presence approach applies in the case of youth mentoring. To illustrate the principles of the presence approach in practice, we will recount the stories of three young people who have taken part in the Big Brothers Big Sisters programme in Ireland. All three young people were currently or had previously lived in state care.

The Foróige Big Brothers Big Sisters programme matches an adult volunteer to a young person (aged between 10 and 18) of the same gender. The aim of the programme is to facilitate the development of a caring and supportive friendship that will reinforce the positive development of the young person. The programme operates within the voluntary sector but works with a range of young people, including those identified as being at high risk, such as young people in residential and foster care and separated youth seeking asylum in Ireland (McGregor, Lynch, & Brady, 2017).

The narratives recounted here are drawn from a research study we conducted to explore the perspectives of young people in care regarding their experiences of mentoring. Detailed one to one narrative style interviews were conducted with 13 young people who are currently or were previously participants in the Big Brothers and Big Sisters youth mentoring programme while in care. The core aim of the study was to explore how young people describe and interpret the significance of their relationship with their mentor and its impact on their overall life and care experience. A narrative style methodology was adopted because it allows people to tell stories about their lives in a relatively organic way, using their own words (Hill & Dallos, 2011). Further detail on the study aims, methodology, and findings can be found in Brady et al. (2020).

For the purposes of this chapter, extracts from the narratives of three young people – Sarah, Lily, and Sean – are presented in their own words. The rationale for doing so is to allow an understanding of how the mentor fitted into the overall life of the young person. Their narratives illustrate how their lives have been shaped by events that occurred in the multiple systems with which they interact, including their birth families, foster families, schools, and social services. While some young people were coping and doing well, others were faced with much more challenging situations, whereby difficult and often painful experiences in their family and home lives had implications for their capacity to cope and thrive in other settings such as school and community. The young people describe what it meant for them to have a mentor in their lives.

We now move on to focus on how Sarah, Lily, and Sean described their mentoring relationships, before reflecting on how mentoring resonates with a 'presence approach'.

Sarah's story

Sarah (24) came to Ireland from Uganda when she was 12 with her parents and sister. A year after arriving, the family experienced issues and she and her sister were placed in care. They lived in a variety of residential homes. Around this time, Sarah was matched with Ciara as part of the BBBS programme. Almost 15 years after their initial match, Sarah and Ciara are still regularly in touch. Sarah spoke about the difficulties of adjusting to life in a new country, her changed family situation and dealing with frequent placement moves in the care system. In this context, Sarah valued Ciara as being someone she could rely on for support in the midst of constant change.

> First of all we were new in the country, the culture was different, the people were different and we were just brought into this home where we were just living with people that we didn't know. Somebody suggested that it would be a really good idea to have a Big Sister, to have that stability, somebody that you can you meet once a week and talk to you and so they introduced me to Ciara.
>
> The first time I met her I didn't know her before so I was a bit shy but then after a few meetings, I got comfortable with her. So we would do like random things, we would go walking, Ciara liked walking so we would go walking together and then we would go to town and we looked at magazines, we went into restaurants and had like maybe a smoothie. So just different stuff and as the time progressed then she would invite me over to her house and then we would cook something from my own country just to try and learn more about each other. So it wasn't like fixed so we did anything that we felt like doing and it was very enjoyable because it wasn't pre planned or anything at the end of it we have a conversation, how are you getting on? Is there anything that is bothering you? And we just have normal conversations like checking in basically. So that consistency was always there ... Even meeting up with her was just an opportunity just to express myself, the concerns that I may have.
>
> I was going to school at that time and because I had just moved to Ireland from Uganda, school was totally different so I was finding it a bit hard to adapt to the school environment because the people there were

not people that I was used to. But she was able to help me out even with practicing my English and just communicating and building up my network with other people.

I did my Junior Cert and I did my Leaving Cert[1] and like so she told me about her college experience but I still didn't know what I really wanted to do. It was great having somebody that was once young like me and had to go through the education system, because she said she didn't know what she wanted to do either. So she goes even if you don't know what you want to do it's not really a problem. So it was more like ok yes I can express exactly how I'm feeling without somebody saying no, that's not a good choice. So it was basically ok that's fine if you don't know what you want to do. So she did inspire me that you don't have to know exactly what you want to do, it's just about making those choices that will lead you to a better future. So she was always that kind of person that yes, ok that's fine if you don't know but make decisions that will lead you towards the future that you want for yourself. So build a foundation for yourself.

She was just always a positive person and also there was like she was this kind of person that just wasn't only interested in me as an individual but also interested in my family so like my sister, she would be as much invested in her. Or even when we were having immigration issues and stuff like that she put herself forward, like is there anything that I can do? You know? Not many people can do that you know? She paid for my first immigration card in Ireland. She didn't have to do that, you know? And I remember one time at Christmas we were in the home and then she came first in the morning with her husband with Christmas stuff, like who would think of, like on Christmas people are just thinking about their family and thinking about themselves but the fact that she was so unselfish. She didn't have to do that, showing up in that house on Christmas morning. Those kind of memories will always you know stand by me. Just authenticity is like, has really even shaped me as a person.

We were dealing with a lot of social workers and stuff like that so most of the time the conversation was written down but with Ciara it wasn't ... When we were going through immigration process and stuff like that everything we said was documented and whether it is for advantage or disadvantage it didn't matter, it was just documented you know?

She wasn't in it for that ... just having the conversation like a child would have a conversation with her mother knowing that it's not being recorded somewhere.

If she wasn't there I probably wouldn't have gotten so many opportunities that I've gotten ... there's so many doors that has opened for me, so many opportunities, so many people I've met that if I hadn't known Ciara I wouldn't have met them you know?

Lily's story

Lily (14) lives in family foster care with her aunt and uncle, who also have three small boys under the age of eight. She said their house is "just crazy". Lily's mother is currently undergoing drugs treatment and she described her relationship with her Dad as "complicated". Lily values her match as somewhere that is just for her; she uses it to talk about her feelings about her family situation. The match has helped her to deal with what is going on in her life.

> So then I have Olivia (mentor) and I just talk to her. I'm able just to go "waah" and just spill everything out. Like even just I'm fighting with my friends or I'm in a bad mood today because this and this and this that happened or I got grounded or something or like anything like. She's actually really helped me with my Dad situation because like I don't live with my Dad and like it's just very complicated time. She's just been there and was able to talk and go on and go on like. I've tried counselling, does not help, art therapy, doesn't help and I feel like this does help. Because she's not like a counsellor. I think when I think they're a counsellor I don't talk. I don't know, I just don't. I don't like it. So I feel like this is more like a friendship kind of thing where it's made for people who can just talk. It's kind of easy going and you go coffee places and you do baking and cooking and she doesn't write things down or anything. She just, we just go with it.
>
> It's like going for a cup of coffee, just talking or like talking about my future and stuff. Like even like the time we baked. it's just fun like. And just talking. We used to go running but kind of we both got lazy so we stopped that … We went on these runs, we ran a 5K and then I ended up winning the fastest time under 18s girls and I got a fifty euro voucher and I was very proud of myself and Olivia was very proud of me as well!
>
> And she's like such a good role model. I actually feel like I'm going to follow in her footsteps. She's 32 and she owns her own house and it's a big apartment. She has a good job and she goes on holidays for her job once a month.
>
> She is a part of my life but she's not part of like all the drama, all the care stuff that I go through all the stuff. And it's just someone I can talk to about literally anything like. I've been in BBBS four years. That's such a long time.
>
> I don't think I could handle everything that's going on right now, like being in care and having all the problems and all … but like with Big Brother Big Sister it's changed me because now I don't bottle up my feelings. I've become a better person. I'm becoming a better person because it's changed me in how the way I look now. I haven't noticed anything in particular how it's changed me but in my head, in my feelings if I didn't have Olivia I don't know who I would be able to talk to. … Olivia comes and takes me out so I'm getting away from all the stress and it's made me not that stressed.

Sean's story

Sean is 18 and just finished secondary school. He has been living with his foster family since he was 6 years old. He is planning to start an apprenticeship soon and intends to move on to live independently. Sean was matched with Stephen for 4 years. They played squash on their first meeting and have been playing it every week since. Sean sees Stephen who is an entrepreneur, as a role model and feels that he has become a lot more sociable since taking part in BBBS. Seeing Sean on the phone, making business calls, and dealing with people helped him to realise that talking to people is "no big deal".

> I was 14 I think when I started with BBBS. Stephen (mentor) was like, "what do you want to do?" and I was like, sure I might as well try squash. Gave it a go and we're playing it since every time we meet. I taught him every rule and every different way to hit the ball; I showed him everything about it. He loves it now.
>
> It made a big difference because like I was sitting at home pretty much the whole time doing nothing other than at the weekends I'd meet my friend but that was only for like one day for a couple of hours. But meeting up with Stephen then during the week was great to get out and get a bit of exercise. And social time as well; I wasn't going to crack up! Someone to have the craic (fun) with.
>
> He was a great influence with his company like. He done really well with that, he's very successful. He's saying like just get through your apprenticeship and go out on your own as soon as you can. Once we finish up with Big Brother Big Sister thing we're still going to meet and play squash as much as we can.
>
> I just didn't connect with social workers you know. I don't like talking to them at all. Even at the review meetings; when I was at them I rarely said anything. But I'd tell Stephen anything. If I needed to yeah I would have talked to him about stuff, yeah … I'd trust him with anything you know … Someone that can understand what I'm talking about. I could text Stephen now and he'd be there to talk even though he probably would be working he'd still try his best to talk to me.
>
> Before I met Stephen I was very socially awkward like; I wouldn't really talk to anybody much but now I'd just go up to anybody and talk to them you know. I'd say it boosted my confidence more with like going to work and getting a job and having a decent life and to improve my social skills. Like when he's with me, sometimes he has to be working as well; he's supposed to be working at home but when he's meeting me he just still works and he's talking about all the people he'd be talking to and ringing them and everything and they'd be ringing him. He'd be sending emails and texts, all sorts. Talking to people all the time and sure why not? It's not that big of a deal.

Drawing on the work of Baart (2002) and Kuis et al. (2015), we have developed four core characteristics of a presence approach in youth mentoring. Mentors as presence practitioners:

1. Are there for the young person. Take time to get to know them. Listen attentively.
2. Are willing to share their own selves, to relax, and be authentic.
3. Don't have a fixed agenda with regard to what the young person needs. They respond intuitively to what the young person brings up. Although not problem-focused, their involvement may lead to problem-solving.
4. Focus on strengths, are non-judgemental/non-critical, strive to affirm the fundamental dignity of the person.

We now draw on the three narratives to illustrate how these principles were illustrated in the mentoring relationships experienced by the young people in our study.

Are there for the young person: take time to get to know them – listen attentively

A feature of presence practitioners is that they "are unhurried, take their time and grant time to the other" (Kuis et al., 2015). Young people taking part in our research described the low key activities that they and their mentors did together, which were experienced as enjoyable and relaxed. Some liked to do sports together while others preferred more passive activities such as hanging out, going for walks, going shopping, or going to cafes. These everyday interactions were undertaken without any particular objective in mind. That such regular support is integrated into daily activities is a feature of the presence approach, whereby interactions between the presence practitioner and the people he or she is supporting take place "on the go and not according to a strict schedule, or in the confidence of a quiet office" (Baart, 2002).

In the context of these activities, the young people had the opportunity to talk to their mentors about normative and challenging issues in their lives, which in turn helped them to deal with problems and stress in their daily lives. There is a sense from the young people's narratives that they trusted their mentors and could share with them what was on their minds. Over the years of their relationships, their mentors were present to share in difficult and joyful situations. Sarah described her mentor paying for her immigration card while Lily spoke of her mentor being so proud when she won a prize for running. This capacity of demonstrating confelicity which is experiencing joy in seeing the happiness and success of others can be seen as an important characteristic of youth mentoring relationships. While the mentor is there to share in good times (confelicity) or bad times (crisis), there are also times when presence mentoring is more neutral, in other words when there is not much happening for the mentee. The young people emphasised the consistency of support available from their mentors; the term "always there" was used frequently. Mentors had clearly conveyed to these young people that they were important to them and that they could be relied on in times of need.

Are willing to share their own selves, relax, be authentic, "let their hair down"

Kuis et al. (2015) describe presence practitioners as being willing to "let their armour down" and "genuinely enter into the presence of the other". In general, mentors were described as being relaxed, and easy to talk to. Part of the reason the mentor was perceived positively in this way is that they generally do activities together that they both enjoy, which makes the conversation more relaxed and less pressurised. Lily described how she and her mentor Olivia used to go running before they "both got lazy", which suggests that they were honest with each other about their feelings. Sean's mentor had never played squash before but was willing to be taught squash by Sean, which led to their developing a shared love for the sport. Similarly, Sarah spoke of how Ciara loved walking and that they spent a lot of time walking. Ciara invited her to her house and they did cooking together. Sean spoke of how his mentor Stephen might be on the phone to clients during their meetings. Seeing Stephen interacting with clients helped Sean to become more sociable and realise that talking wasn't so difficult.

Both Sarah and Lily mentioned that their mentors did not write down anything about their meetings, and that the communication was just between them. Formal processes in social services can mean that young people have their family and personal issues documented and shared with others, arguably losing control over their own story of who they are and what is important to them. Lily and Sarah's narratives show how commonly they had experienced this instrumental form of helping, which they felt was inauthentic. Sarah used the word "authentic" to describe Ciara's interactions with her compared to those of other professionals.

Don't have a fixed agenda with regard to what the young person needs: they respond intuitively to what the young person brings up – although not problem-focused, their involvement may lead to problem-solving

One of the key characteristics of presence practitioners are that they have no fixed agenda and are "engaged with the life, the tempo, the rhythm and the language field of the other" (Kuis et al., 2015, p. 177). According to Kuis et al. (2015), presence practitioners are open for what possibly requires their attention and dedication and respond open-mindedly to it, which helps to connect the practitioner with the other. Furthermore, presence practitioners "learn to perceive the world from the perspective of the other", understanding what is important for the other and why.

It was apparent from the narratives of Lily, Sarah, and Sean that their mentors allowed them to tell their own story and got to know them on their own terms. Their relationships helped them to flourish as they people they were, rather than encouraging them towards a path or outcome that they did not want. As she developed trust with Ciara, Sarah was able to open up to her about the challenges she faced at school and to get help from Ciara with speaking English more clearly and deciding on an educational path. Ciara responded to issues that were happening in Sarah's life and offered help as required. The support Sarah received was thus timely and tailored to her self-identified needs. Similarly, Lily appreciated that she could use her mentoring relationship in the way she needed, which for her was a space to express her feelings about her complicated family life and the struggles and pressures she experienced at school. Engaging in activities while talking worked much better for her than counselling or art therapy had done previously. Likewise, Sean's mentor did not push any agenda but was there to talk during their weekly game of squash as needed. As a result, Sean developed a strong trust in him and said he was willing to confide in him about things that were important to him and was willing to take career advice from him. These examples reflect Baart's (2002) reference to presence practitioners as participating "in the handling of existential questions and critical moments of decision" (p. 2), which are shared after trust has developed. They also illustrate how problem-solving can occur without a direct focus on "problems".

Focus on strengths, are non-judgemental/non-critical, strive to affirm the fundamental dignity of the person

Kuis et al. (2015, p. 177) posit that presence practitioners connect to the reality of the world of the other – they "leave to the other what belongs to the other and do not diminish, expropriate or overrule it". In this regard, the presence approach can be seen to align with a strengths perspective, which, rather than focusing on risk and problems, seeks to work with people to identify and build on their strengths and resources (Saleebey, 2009). Importantly, practitioners working from a strengths perspective avoid preconceptions or stereotypes, choosing instead to work with individuals to understand their experiences and aspirations and support them to achieve them. In doing so, the dignity of the person is affirmed (Baart, 2002).

Sean's account of how he taught his mentor Stephen "every rule and every different way to hit the ball" can be seen as an illustration of a strength's perspective in action. It appears that Stephen intuitively built on Sean's strengths as a squash player and affirmed his dignity by respecting, learning from, and deriving great enjoyment from Sean's expertise. Sarah's comment "I can express exactly how I'm feeling without somebody saying no, that's not a good choice" speaks to the importance of a uncritical approach for her. She also describes how her mentor Ciara encouraged her to cook something from her own country, thus affirming and valuing Sarah's cultural heritage. These examples resonate with previous research positing that mentoring which focuses on emphasising youth assets, rather than their deficits, is likely to be more successful (Higley, Walker, Bishop, & Fritz, 2016; Liang, Bogat, & Duffy, 2013). Similarly, social support theory underlines the importance of the perceived quality of the support available; people prefer helpers who are non-demeaning (Bolger & Amarel, 2007).

Conclusion

In this chapter, we have argued that a presence approach can be seen as having relevance and value for youth mentoring programmes. Building on Baart's (2002) conceptualisation, the "presence approach" means that the worker or volunteer is fully attentive to and "there for" the mentee. The "presence mentors" take time to get to know their mentee and what matters to them, while respecting and upholding the dignity of the person. While not focused on problem-solving, mentors adopting a presence approach can support young people to cope and thrive in ways that are meaningful to them, as illustrated by our case vignettes.

We argue that pure, agenda-free friendships in mentoring need to be fully appreciated by professional social services, voluntary organisations, policy-makers, and academics. The approach can be seen to have particular value for young people who have had complex and difficult lives, such as young people in the care system, who may have many professionals involved in their lives offering "instrumental" forms of support. We acknowledge the limitations of our small sample but believe that the concept has sufficient value to merit further research and theorisation. Furthering this approach brings with it an implicit demand to move from an outcome focus in mentoring programmes towards a more organic, caring, and human intention (Prieto-Flores & Feu, 2018). When recruiting, training, and supervising mentors for children and young people, mentoring organisations should pay attention to the characteristics of a "presence approach", which have been identified as important by young people in this and previous studies.

Note

1. Junior Cert and Leaving Certificate are Irish state examinations undertaken at approximately ages 15 and 18, respectively.

References

Ahrens, K. R., Dubois, D. L., Garrison, M., Spencer, R., Richardson, L. P., & Lozano, P. (2011). Qualitative exploration of relationships with important non-parental adults in the lives of youth in foster care. *Children and Youth Services Review, 33*(6), 1012–1023.

Baart, A. (2002). The presence approach, an introductory sketch of a practice. Retrieved from http://www.presentie.nl/publicaties/item/download/246%20[8%20Mar%202002]

Baart, A., & Vosman, F. (2011). Relationship based care and recognition. Part one: Sketching good care from the theory of presence and five entries. In C. Leget, C. Gastmans, & M. Verkerk (Eds.), *Care, compassion and recognition: An ethical discussion* (pp. 183–200). Leuven, Belgium: Peters.

Beresford, P., Croft, S., & Adshead, L. (2007). 'We don't see her as a social worker': A service user case study of the importance of the social worker's relationship and humanity. *British Journal of Social Work*, 38(7), 1388–1407.

Bilson, A., Featherstone, B., & Martin, K. (2017). How child protection's 'investigative turn' impacts on poor and deprived communities. *Family Law Journal*, 47(4), 416–419.

Bolger, N., & Amarel, D. (2007). Effects of social support visibility on adjustment to stress: Experimental evidence. *Journal of Personality and Social Psychology*, 92(3), 458–475.

Brady, B., Dolan, P., & Canavan, J. (2017). 'He told me to calm down and all that': A qualitative study of social support types in a youth mentoring programme. *Child and Family Social Work*, 22(1), 266–274.

Brady, B., Dolan, P., & McGregor, C. (2020). *Mentoring for young people in care and leaving care: Theory, policy and practice*. London: Routledge.

Colley, H. (2003). *Mentoring for social inclusion*. London: Routledge Falmer.

DeWit, D. J., DuBois, D., Erdem, G., Larose, S., Lipman, E. L., & Spencer, R. (2016). Mentoring relationship closures in Big Brothers Big Sisters community mentoring programs: Patterns and associated risk factors. *American Journal of Community Psychology*, 57(1–2), 60–72.

Gettings, P. E., & Wilson, S. R. (2014). Examining commitment and relational maintenance in formal youth mentoring relationships. *Journal of Social and Personal Relationships*, 31(8), 1089–1115.

Golightley M., & Holloway M (2018). The personal and professional: Towards a more holistic knowledge base. *British Journal of Social Work*, 48 (1–7), 1831–1835.

Habermas, J. (2015). *The theory of communicative action: Lifeworld and systems, a critique of functionalist reason* (Vol. 2). Hoboken, NJ: John Wiley & Sons.

Higley, E., Walker, S. C., Bishop, A. S., & Fritz, C. (2016). Achieving high quality and long-lasting matches in youth mentoring programmes: A case study of mentoring. *Child & Family Social Work*, 21(2), 240–248.

Hill, K., & Dallos, R. (2011). Young people's stories of self-harm: A narrative study. *Clinical Child Psychology and Psychiatry*, 17(3), 459–475.

Horn, J. P., & Spencer, R. (2018). Natural mentoring to support the establishment of permanency for youth in foster care. In E. Trejos-Castillo, & N. Trevino-Schafer (Eds.), *Handbook of Foster Youth*. New York, NY: Routledge.

Hyslop, I. (2018). Neoliberalism and social work identity. *European Journal of Social Work*, 21(1), 20–31.

Jackson, R., Brady, B., Forkan, C., Tierney, E., & Kennan, D. (2018). *Collective participation of children in care: A formative evaluation of the Tusla/EPIC foster care action groups*. Galway: UNESCO Child and Family Research Centre, NUI Galway.

Kuis, E. E., Goossensen, A., Van Dijke, J., & Baart, A. J. (2015). Self-report questionnaire for measuring presence: Development and initial validation. *Scandinavian Journal of Caring Sciences Methods and Methodologies*, 29, 173–182.

Liang, B., Bogat, A., & Duffy, N. (2013). *Gender in mentoring relationships. Handbook of youth mentoring*. Thousand Oaks, CA: Sage.

McGregor, C. (2019). Paradigm framework for social work theory for early 21st century practice. *The British Journal of Social Work*. https://doi.org/10.1093/bjsw/bcz006

McGregor, C., Lynch, M., & Brady, B. (2017). Youth mentoring as a form of support for children and young people at risk: Insights from research and practice. In P. Dolan, & N. Frost (Eds.), *The Routledge handbook of global child welfare* (pp. 345–357). London: Routledge.

Meier, R. (2008). *Youth mentoring: A good thing?* Surrey: Centre for Policy Studies.

Munro, E. (2011). *The Munro review of child protection*. London: Stationery Office.

Munson, M. R., Smalling, S. E., Spencer, R., Scott, L. D., & Tracy, E. M. (2010). A steady presence in the midst of change: Non-kin natural mentors in the lives of older youth exiting foster care. *Children and Youth Services Review, 32*(4), 527–535.

Philip, K., & Spratt, J. (2007). *A synthesis of published research on mentoring and befriending*. Manchester: Mentoring and Befriending Foundation.

Prieto-Flores, Ò., & Feu, J. F. (2018). What type of impact could social mentoring programs have? An exploration of the existing assessments and a proposal of an analytical framework. *Pedagogia Social, 31*, 149–162.

Rhodes, J. E. (2005). A model of youth mentoring. In D. L. DuBois, & M. J. Karcher (Eds.), *Handbook of youth mentoring* (pp. 30–43). Thousand Oaks, CA: Sage Publications.

Ryan, P., Ford, R., Beadsmore, A., & Muijen, M. (1999). The Sainsbury centre case management study. *British Journal of Social Work, 29*, 97–125.

Saleebey, D. (2009). *The Strengths Perspective in Social Work Practice*. Boston: Allyn & Bacon.

Silke, C., Brady, B., & Dolan, P. (2019a). *Relational dynamics in youth mentoring: A mixed methods study*. Galway: UNESCO Child & Family Research Centre.

Silke, C., Brady, B., & Dolan, P. (2019b). Relational dynamics in formal youth mentoring programmes: A longitudinal investigation into the association between relationship satisfaction and youth outcomes. *Children and Youth Services Review, 104*. https://doi.org/10.1016/j.childyouth.2019.05.020

Spencer, R. (2012). A working model of mentors' contributions to youth mentoring relationship quality: Insights from research on psychotherapy. *LEARNing Landscapes, 5*(2), 295–312.

Stein, M. (2012). *Young people leaving care: Supporting pathways to adulthood*. London: Jessica Kingsley Publishers.

Sudbery, J. (2002). Key features of therapeutic social work: The use of relationship. *Journal of Social Work Practice, 6*(2), 149–162.

Van Dam, L., Smit, D., Wildschut, B., Branje, S. J. T., Rhodes, J. E., Assink, M., & Stams, G. J. J. M. (2018). Does natural mentoring matter? A multilevel meta-analysis on the association between natural mentoring and youth outcomes. *American Journal of Community Psychology, 62*(1–2), 203–220.

Chapter 3

The role of mentoring and service learning in youth's critical consciousness and social change efforts

Bernadette Sánchez, Beth S. Catlett, Lidia Y. Monjaras-Gaytan, Rebecca McGarity-Palmer, Amy J. Anderson, C. Lynn Liao, and Christopher B. Keys

The role of mentors in young people's lives has been the subject of national attention and scholarly interest for several decades. Most recently, scholars, community activists, and advocates have begun to critique conventional approaches to mentoring and mentoring scholarship and argue for the benefits of applying a more critical theoretical lens. The current chapter builds on this scholarly trend. We begin by briefly summarising current critiques of traditional approaches to mentoring programmes and research. We then move to the focus of our work – the role of mentors and mentoring in helping to develop critical consciousness (CC) among young people. CC is a process in which individuals critically analyse their social conditions and act to change these conditions (Freire, 1973; Watts et al., 2011). Youth mentoring is a meaningful relationship between a child/adolescent and an adult who provides support and guidance for the benefit of the young person (DuBois, Portillo, Rhodes, Silverthorn, & Valentine, 2011). Adult mentors are well positioned to guide and support youth in efforts to develop their CC and to work toward social change. However, there is limited research on the role of mentors in the development of youth CC. Thus, in addition to providing a literature review of this limited body of scholarship, we also examine the role of other important adults in young people's lives. Our chapter also focuses on critical approaches to service learning – primarily focused on college students – to inform ongoing and future work on the role of supportive adults in the development of CC among young people. Finally, recommendations for future research and practice in empowering mentoring are provided.

Moving toward a critical perspective in youth mentoring

Historically, youth mentoring programmes in the United States have failed to take a critical approach to addressing systems of power and inequality and creating social change for youth being served. Similarly, with a few notable exceptions (e.g. Hall, 2015; Weiston-Serdan, 2017), the scholarly literature on youth mentoring has generally lacked a critical theoretical approach, and rather has focused on conventional ways in which a supportive intergenerational relationship can promote improved developmental outcomes in youth. Thus, issues of power, privilege, and oppression, as well as systemic inequalities have not been fully attended to in existing literature (Albright, Hurd, & Hussain, 2017). Scholars recently have begun to highlight how this conventional approach to mentoring has the potential to reproduce rather than reduce structural inequalities (Albright et al., 2017; Schwartz & Rhodes, 2016; Weiston-Serdan, 2017). This traditional model too often relies on a false understanding of need, placing the focus on individuals and on mitigating individual deficits. This model does not attend to complex dominant sociopolitical systems that, on a societal level, impact entire communities and rob individuals of access and opportunity. Moreover, implementation of a conventional mentoring model comes with significant, if subtle, risks that privilege those doing the mentoring relative to the young people who are being served.

Critics point out that traditional mentoring models do not go deep enough, stopping short of a collaborative exploration between mentors and mentees of the complex sociopolitical dynamics that underlie larger social problems (Weiston-Serdan, 2017). Mentoring approaches too often take a Eurocentric, individualistic, middle class, hierarchical approach to mentoring. Some of the large mentoring programmes in the United States, such as Big Brothers Big Sisters, primarily serve low-income youth of colour (Valentino & Wheeler, 2013), while the majority of mentors are White. In a US survey of 1,451 youth mentoring programmes, it was found that 86% of the mentees served in their programmes were youth of colour, while the majority (53%) of volunteers who served as mentors were White (Garringer, McQuillen, & McDaniel, 2017). An underlying assumption in the mentoring field is that a one-on-one relationship between a middle-class White mentor and a poor youth of colour will help the mentee escape their circumstances through the opportunities provided by the mentor and through learning skills to adapt to a predominantly white society. This assumption perpetuates the white saviour or missionary mentality so common in education (Freire, 1985), community service and humanitarian efforts in the United States and around the world (e.g. Help to Save campaign in the United Kingdom, HM Treasury, 2016). Researchers and educators have critiqued the assumptions and approaches of the youth mentoring field by calling out this approach as inconsistent with the cultural values of the youth typically served in these programmes (Sánchez & Colón, 2005). In addition, they argue that a critical mentoring approach is needed in order to understand and change the systemic forces that have created the oppressive conditions in which many low-income youth of colour live (Weiston-Serdan, 2017).

A promising expansion of traditional approaches to mentoring is to view these youth-adult relationships as vehicles for expanding young people's CC

(Liang, Spencer, West, & Rappaport, 2013), and researchers have recently begun to discuss and explore this potential (Albright et al., 2017; Weiston-Serdan, 2017). Further, the CC of college students serving as mentors in service-learning programmes – as well as college students involved in service-learning experiences more generally – is shown to be impacted by cantering classroom discussions and reflections on power, privilege, and oppression. This literature on critical service-learning can push the youth mentoring field to take a more critical and ultimately empowering approach to mentoring research and practices.

Critical consciousness

With its roots in Brazil, the concept of *conscientização* (or CC) refers to a process of social analysis and action that is developed from the bottom-up through education and dialogue (Freire, 1973). CC has been applied to diverse groups in North America and is considered a key component of youth civic engagement (Watts et al., 2011), youth organising (Kirshner & Ginwright, 2012), and youth activism (Diemer & Rapa, 2016). Empowerment theory and research has often placed CC at the heart of developing psychological empowerment on the individual level (Keys, McConnell, Motley, Liao, & McAuliff, 2017; Zimmerman, 1990). Yet methods for fostering the development of CC have been limited as has research regarding CC.

CC is comprised of critical reflection and action (Watts et al., 2011). Critical reflection refers to a critical analysis of social, economic, and political structures that serve as oppressive barriers to justice (Watts & Flanagan, 2007). Critical action is the participation in individual or collective social action to change perceived injustices (Diemer, Rapa, Park, & Perry, 2017). Critical reflection is generally viewed as a precursor to critical action, assuming that people need to gain awareness of injustices as a motivator in order to engage in social action (Watts et al., 2011). However, Freire (1970) emphasises the iterative nature of CC; once people begin to participate in social action, they then continue to gain a deeper understanding of structural injustices and engage in more complex critical reflection.

Researchers have examined other interrelated concepts when conducting investigations on CC, including political efficacy, self-efficacy, and sociopolitical control. Political efficacy is regarded as a component of CC, and refers to one's perceived capacity to create political and social change (Diemer & Rapa, 2016); and self-efficacy is typically regarded as a core element of psychological empowerment (Keys et al., 2017). Sociopolitical control is the extent to which individuals perceive that they can affect social change through political participation and social action (Watts et al., 2011). These various constructs emerge when examining the role of non-parental adults in youth's CC below.

Role of mentoring and supportive adults in youth's critical consciousness

Historically, CC is rooted in Paulo Freire's work in education and the concept of conscientizaçao, which refers to a process of social analysis and action that is developed from the bottom-up through education and dialogue (Freire, 1973). Freire (1970) rejected the banking concept of education, in which students are passive "depositories" and teachers "deposit" knowledge. Instead, Freire (1970) advocated for a problem-posing education that leads to liberation. Specifically, rather than information being merely transferred from teacher to student, there is an emphasis on breaking down the hierarchical student-teacher relationship through dialogue. This dialogue enables individuals to critically reflect on their position within and choose the appropriate actions to transform their world. In line with this idea, Freire and education theorists (1997) conceptualise mentoring as one in which both mentors and mentees engage in reciprocal and collaborative learning with one another, which means that mentees are agents of their own learning and social change efforts.

Drawing upon Freire's views, Diemer and Li (2011) posit that CC develops when youth are provided support and guidance to reflect upon and challenge social injustices. Scholars have noted that a key factor in the development of CC among youth is when adults facilitate dialogue and awareness of social injustices (Diemer, Kauffman, Koenig, Trahan, & Hsieh, 2006). Further, the youth civic engagement literature has emphasised the roles of non-parental adults, such as teachers (Godfrey & Grayman, 2014; Seider, Tamerat, Clark, & Soutter, 2017) and out-of-school time staff at community-based organisations, in youth's civic and political development (Zeldin, Christens, & Powers, 2013).

Mentors are well positioned to support the development of young people's CC (Albright et al., 2017). Mentoring includes volunteer relationships in which an older volunteer mentor is matched to work with a mentee (DuBois et al., 2011) or natural mentoring relationships that develop organically with nonfamilial (e.g. teachers, neighbour) or familial adults (e.g. older cousin, aunt) in youth's social networks (Zimmerman, Bingenheimer, & Behrendt, 2005). A suggested shift in the mentoring field is to move from a traditional hierarchical and therapeutic approach toward socially transformative youth-adult interactions and relationships in order to create social change (Liang et al., 2013). Using positive youth development and community psychology perspectives, Liang et al. (2013) argue that mentors should support youth in their CC and social activism by engaging in youth-adult partnerships (Zeldin, Larson, Camino, & O'Connor, 2005). Similar to the Freire model of education (Freire et al., 1997), youth-adult partnerships are reciprocal relationships that involve sharing power, collaborating on tasks and activities, learning from one another, addressing societal barriers, and emphasising youth voice.

This kind of critical mentoring requires that mentors participate in trainings that teach them how to work with mentees in youth-adult partnerships and to become aware of how their own power and privilege impact their interactions with and views of mentees (Liang et al., 2013). Other mentoring researchers have also reiterated the importance of training mentors to make them aware of their own biases and assumptions and of the role of power, privilege, and oppression in their own lives as well as in their mentees' lives (Albright et al., 2017).

In fact, research shows promising evidence, albeit correlational, of the role of trainings in mentors' sociopolitical awareness and in their understanding of how environmental factors (e.g. institutional barriers) influence mentees and their families (Anderson, Sánchez, Meyer, & Sales, 2018). In an evaluation of a social justice training that included critical reflection about oppression, privilege, and systemic social issues for volunteer mentors and programme staff, researchers found that sociopolitical awareness increased for mentors who participated in a training tailored to the needs of their mentee (i.e. young Black boys and men; Anderson et al., 2018). The findings suggest that when provided space for critical reflection, mentors' CC can also be facilitated. Training mentors is a necessary first step towards helping them to support youth's CC.

Although scholarly attention to the ways in which adults can support the development of CC among youth has begun to emerge, few researchers have specifically examined the role of non-parental adults in youth's CC, and the findings are mixed. A study of 299 Malaysian youth (15–24 years of age) in after-school and community programmes found that more youth voice in programme decision-making predicted more sociopolitical control, above and beyond demographic characteristics, school connectedness, religious community involvement, family cohesion, and parental monitoring (Krauss et al., 2014). However, youth's report of supportive adult relationships in their community did not significantly predict sociopolitical control. In a 2-year study of 50 adolescents and 40 staff from a community-based organisation, researchers investigated characteristics of youth-adult relationships that helped youth develop as social activists (O'Donoghue & Strobel, 2007). Analyses revealed three characteristics of these relationships: (a) supportive, (b) egalitarian, and (c) embedded in public action. Supportive relationships comprised of genuine caring and open and honest feedback, and adults positively challenged youth. The relationships were also egalitarian; they were nonhierarchical, democratic, collaborative, youth-centred, and reciprocal. Finally, staff-youth relationships were embedded in public action. They focused on meaningful public action work and engaged in public projects together. These studies demonstrate the ways that adults can support and interact with adolescents to help them develop CC.

Researchers have also examined the role of teachers and school principals in young people's CC (Diemer & Li, 2011; Godfrey & Grayman, 2014). In a study of poor and working class, racially/ethnically diverse young people between the ages of 15 and 25, researchers did *not* find that teacher sociopolitical support (i.e. emphasising forms of injustice [e.g. racism], different opinions and perspectives about political/social issues, and the formation of students' opinions about social issues) was significantly related to either youth's sense of sociopolitical control or social action participation (e.g. participated in a protest or march, signed a petition about a political issue; Diemer & Li, 2011). A limitation of this study, however, is that the authors did not assess critical reflection; perhaps teacher sociopolitical support is related to students' critical reflection of social issues. Likewise, a cross-sectional, nationally representative sample of low-income, 12th-grade students of colour ($N = 2,078$) in the United States examined school principal-reported support for democratic participation (i.e. student societal involvement and practice of citizenship, participation in student government, awareness of social issues, and promotion of moral and values education; Diemer, Hsieh, & Pan, 2009). The authors did not find a significant association between principal support and students' motivation to change sociopolitical inequity in their community (Diemer et al., 2009). Perhaps the role of school principals would have been significant if they specifically provided direct support for student involvement in critical sociopolitical action.

Another study examined teachers' sociopolitical support by examining open classroom climate, the extent that teachers "foster discussion of controversial issues, encourage students to present diverse opinions and emphasize respect of those opinions from teachers and students" (Godfrey & Grayman, 2014, p. 1803), which may allow for critical dialogue and reflection (Freire, 1973). In contrast to the previous studies on teacher and principal sociopolitical support (Diemer et al., 2009; Diemer & Li, 2011), this study found that a more open classroom climate was associated with higher sociopolitical efficacy and critical action but not critical reflection among a U.S. sample of 9th-grade students (Godfrey & Grayman, 2014).

Based on the previous research, it seems that simply being supportive of youth, even if the support is around sociopolitical issues, is insufficient in promoting CC (e.g. Diemer et al., 2009; Diemer & Li, 2011; Krauss et al., 2014). Such support may or may not touch upon critical perspectives and power relations in society. Further, youth and adults may need to be actively engaged together on sociopolitical issues. However, given the limited research on the role of mentors and non-parental adults in youth CC, the service-learning literature is also examined to provide further insight in how to promote young people's CC.

Development of critical consciousness among college students via service learning and mentoring

Given the paucity of research on the role of mentors and non-parental adults in youth's CC, it is instructive to consider the service-learning literature on college students' CC development. Young people may experience structured opportunities, such as service learning, that are primed for mentoring relationships in the context of CC building. Service learning is a pedagogical approach that combines academic coursework with civic engagement and personal growth whereby students typically engage in volunteer roles or projects in community settings, and reflect on those experiences within the context of scholarly work in the university classroom (Mitchell, 2007).

The current scholarly trend within service-learning literature parallels the recent emphasis on critical mentoring with youth (Weiston-Serdan, 2017) and has acknowledged the potential social change aspects of the enterprise. More specifically, service learning within higher education has been reconsidered over the last decade with enhanced attention to application of a critical theoretical lens that situates college students' community engagement within systems of social inequality (Mitchell, 2007). A change model of service learning (Bickford & Reynolds, 2002; Boyle-Baise & Langford, 2004; King, 2004) facilitates students' CC. That is, students engage in critical reflection on social problems and consideration of the roles they can play in engaging with communities to create a different, and more equitable, social landscape. By strategically orienting service learning toward social justice in this fashion, college students have the opportunity to develop their CC, in particular developing their critical reflection of the structural inequalities that organise society and the strategic action steps that can yield different outcomes for individuals and communities (Catlett & Proweller, 2015). This literature can inform research and practice on the role of mentors in youth's CC, particularly on mentor training and preparation.

Although a full review of university service-learning literature is beyond the scope of this chapter, it is important to note that the somewhat inconsistent research findings suggest that conclusions remain elusive about the benefit of implementing a change model of service learning. In such a model, CC and the interrogation of power and privilege are emphasised. Research has begun to suggest that centering the relationships among service learning, power, privilege, and critical theoretical frameworks has the potential to shape more equitable relationships and a more just society. Meeting this goal depends on students having destabilising experiences (King, 2004) that force interrogation of taken-for-granted and deeply embedded assumptions about power and privilege.

This opportunity for interrogation, and development of CC, is particularly important given that service-learning students often are from more educationally and socioeconomically privileged positions than the communities in which they serve. Specifically, a majority of students commonly taking service-learning classes are White and middle class, and they typically are placed in service activities in lower income communities of colour (Green, 2001). In that context, the service-learning experience risks being seen as privileged Whites acting benevolently to teach and serve those perceived as lacking the skills to achieve on their own (Dunlap, Scoggin, Green, & Davi, 2007). Thus, similar to what scholars have cautioned in terms of the potential risks in youth mentoring relationships (Albright et al., 2017), there is a significant concern that service learning could potentially reinforce one's privilege if opportunities are not built in for students to critically reflect on their service responsibilities, the basis for their service, and the relationship between their service and the unearned advantage of being relatively privileged to begin with. Accordingly, these scholars have noted that service-learning students need to be given opportunities to examine assumptions, discourses, and practices about power and privilege. This kind of reflection increases the likelihood that students will become more critically conscious. It can develop the possibilities that service learning holds for building more collaborative, equitable, and invested relationships across difference.

Several scholars have suggested that the linkages between service learning, CC, and social justice need to be made explicit to avoid the unintended consequence of doing more harm than good when service falls short of cultivating student awareness of systemic inequality and the need to change existing power imbalances. For instance, Eyler and Giles (1999) found that service learning that includes critical reflection can diminish negative stereotypes and increase tolerance for diversity among service-learning students. These findings prompted service-learning educators to purposefully integrate opportunities for critical reflection about the root causes of social inequities into service-learning experiences. Furthermore, Green (2001, 2003) explored the potential of intentionally incorporating discussion about privilege, particularly around positions of race and class, into service-learning experiences. In her empirical study exploring this potential, Green (2001) examined the experiences of students who tutored middle-school students on a weekly basis in an inner-city community close to the university campus. Although she emphasised the challenges that talking about race and class present for those students in positions of relative privilege, she also reported students' progress in speaking about historically unnamed categories of unearned advantage and conferred dominance (McIntosh, 1988). She further concluded that, although student development can be varied and uneven, the service-learning educational experience can prompt key insights. These include learning about the roots of systemic inequality and holding oneself accountable for working to interrupt relations of exploitation and domination.

Catlett and Proweller (2011, 2015) studied the experience of college students who facilitated a violence prevention and community activism programme with high school-aged youth. Similar to Green (2001), they found service-learning experiences focused on development of CC can cultivate a deeper awareness of the structural and systemic nature of power, privilege, and oppression. Moreover, this emergent understanding has the potential to promote seeing oneself as a change agent, working in collaboration with younger teens to advance social justice.

These findings are also reflected in research that specifically examines college students' roles as mentors to younger populations. More specifically, several studies have emerged from service-learning mentoring programmes in which primarily White, middle-class undergraduate students serve as mentors to primarily low-income, Black high school students (Hughes, Boyd, & Dykstra, 2010; Hughes et al., 2012). A service-learning mentoring programme consisted of social justice training for mentors through their course content, mentoring youth on site, ongoing reflections, and class discussions (Hughes et al., 2010, 2012). Research findings suggest that ongoing training, discussion, mentoring, and critical reflection led to increased CC about racial and economic inequalities and the ways privilege operates in the mentors' lives. The university student mentors were able to identify and challenge assumptions they had made before working in the programme (Hughes et al., 2012). These early assumptions were grounded in stereotypes too routinely applied to historically marginalized communities and disenfranchised populations (Okun, 2010). Recognising these assumptions is a necessary beginning in an evolution toward CC that can shape their work as mentors with younger individuals.

As these examples illustrate, scholars have identified the positive potential of such a critically-oriented model of service learning that promotes the development of CC among college students. At the same time, however, even this model of service-learning experience itself can leave students "stall(ed) in personal consciousness raising" (Boyle-Baise & Langford, 2004, p. 64) without a CC of the structural reasons for community problems and action steps that can be taken in their service role. Scholars also have discussed the potential to "miseducate students if they walk away from the experience with essentialised notions of the communities with whom they worked" (Hui, 2009, p. 23). In sum, it is necessary for young people to develop both critical reflection and action aimed at structural change and that extends into continued development beyond the service-learning experience.

Discussion and recommendations for future practice and research

The development of CC can be an important building block in the development of psychological empowerment. As the above review of the service-learning literature illustrates, the opportunities and potential risks that have been examined with college student populations are indeed instructive and find parallels within the broader body of research on mentoring and CC. Both the service-learning and youth mentoring literatures discuss the potential for negative outcomes when volunteers (i.e. college students, volunteer mentors) who are typically more educationally and socio-economically privileged and often White and middle class engage with or serve low-income communities of colour. The change model of service learning discussed earlier (Bickford & Reynolds, 2002; Boyle-Baise & Langford, 2004; King, 2004) seeks to mitigate the potential for negative outcomes, and can be instructive to the youth mentoring field to inspire practitioners and researchers to consider how mentors can engage in critical reflection on social problems and on their roles in working with communities to create a different, and more equitable, social landscape. Thus, mentors' CC is a necessary first step towards the promotion of young people's CC.

Similar to the service-learning literature, Albright et al. (2017) suggest that we cannot simply rely on mentors' relationships with marginalised youth to spark mentors' CC, but that mentors need to be explicitly trained on social justice issues. Mentor trainings should include structured and ongoing opportunities in which mentors can examine and critically reflect on their own power, privilege and biases and to learn about systems of oppression that marginalise many of the youth served by mentoring programmes (Anderson et al., 2018). Furthermore, mentors may benefit from being taught to partner with youth on CC building activities (Albright et al., 2017; Liang et al., 2013).

This literature review points to suggestions regarding how adults and mentors can engage with youth to promote their CC. Research suggests that simply providing non-parental adult support to young people, even if it is sociopolitical support, is insufficient in promoting CC (e.g. Diemer & Li, 2011). Similar to Freire's (1973) theorising about the central importance of problem-posing education and dialogue, critical reflection, and social action, mentors should be actively exploring with mentees the controversial political and social issues that affect mentees' everyday lives. Some mentoring programme staff and volunteers shy away from having these conversations with youth because they may be afraid of emotionally and politically evocative conversations (Rhodes, 2018). They may not be adequately prepared or trained to facilitate these discussions, or perhaps they believe that adolescents are not concerned about these issues. But research suggests that dialogue and conversation is an avenue towards awakening youth's CC (Diemer et al., 2006; Godfrey & Grayman, 2014). Further, such dialogue creates an opportunity to not only engage in analysis about the structural inequality in our society but to also help young people "process deep and painful emotions" regarding the various inequalities (e.g. racism, classism) that they directly experience (Quiroz-Martínez, HoSang, & Villarosa, 2004, p. 7).

As Freire emphasises in his notion of praxis (1973), mentors should not only engage in critical reflection with youth, but they also should engage in collaborative critical action. As discussed previously, research on the development of youth social activism demonstrates the importance of creating youth–adult relationships that are supportive and egalitarian, and create opportunities for adults to work alongside youth in conducting public action projects (O'Donoghue & Strobel, 2007). Traditional youth mentoring programmes tend to be focused on promoting traditional outcomes in mentees, such as academic achievement, and preventing problem behaviours, such as substance use (e.g. see DuBois et al., 2011). Moving towards a CC perspective in mentoring implies that volunteer mentors should collaborate with youth in analysis of social issues, as well as engage in social action projects that have the potential to directly and positively impact their communities. Youth–adult partnerships that centre both critical reflection and action could have an indirect and positive effect on traditional outcomes (e.g. school grades) that are of interest to youth mentoring programmes.

Moreover, the youth–adult partnership literature (Liang et al., 2013; Zeldin et al., 2005) provides insight in terms of how mentors and youth can collaborate around social activism. Developing a sociopolitically informed approach to mentoring suggests the need for the development of new mentoring models and organisations. For instance, re-focusing traditional mentoring models to more fully centre sociopolitical analysis and action could prompt youth organisations to create new initiatives such as unions and grassroots projects in which youth and adults work in partnership to address pressing community concerns.

This literature review on mentoring and CC also has implications for future research. Conducting participatory action research projects with both youth and adult mentors may be an avenue toward developing effective and innovative critical mentoring models (Weiston-Serdan, 2017). Participatory action research would centre youth voice in the research process and decision-making, and create opportunities for youth and adults to work together on collaborative projects. Moving forward, researchers also would be well advised to further interrogate the links among mentoring, critical reflection, and critical action. For example, research on the ways in which mentor involvement with youth to examine sociopolitical issues, and the ways that these examinations might deepen adolescents' critical reflection, is warranted. In addition, further examination of the bi-directional and iterative relationship between critical reflection and critical action (Watts et al., 2011) will help to deepen our understanding.

Moreover, research to identify specific processes and mechanisms of change is important, in particular to identify the role of specific activities, projects, and types of support that mentors and other non-parental adults should provide to young people to promote the development of CC. We suggest that future research examine the roles of critical dialogue, social advocacy, and collective action as mentors work with youth toward the development of CC, youth leadership, and youth empowerment.

Finally, as discussed above, recent research has produced promising results about the role of mentor training programmes to support sociopolitical awareness and CC among mentors (Anderson et al., 2018). These preliminary research findings suggest that training mentors is a necessary, and vitally important, first step toward helping them to support youth's CC. Thus, the training and CC development of mentors is of central importance for future research. We emphasise the significance of this line of scholarly inquiry, in particular because without critically informed engagement of adult mentors, the mentoring relationship may, however unintentionally, further alienate youth and reinforce structural inequality.

References

Albright, J. N., Hurd, N. M., & Hussain, S. B. (2017). Applying a social justice lens to youth mentoring: A review of the literature and recommendations for practice. *American Journal of Community Psychology*, *59*(3–4), 363–381.

Anderson, A. J., Sánchez, B., Meyer, G., & Sales, B. P. (2018). Supporting adults to support youth: An evaluation of two social justice trainings. *Journal of Community Psychology*, *46*(8), 1092–1106.

Bickford, D. M., & Reynolds, N. (2002). Activism and service-learning: Reframing volunteerism as acts of dissent. *Pedagogy*, *2*(2), 229–252.

Boyle-Baise, M., & Langford, J. (2004). There are children here: Service learning for social justice. *Equity & Excellence in Education*, *37*(1), 55–66.

Catlett, B. S., & Proweller, A. (2011). College students' negotiation of privilege in a community-based violence prevention project. *Michigan Journal of Community Service Learning*, *18*(1), 34–49.

Catlett, B.S., & Proweller, A. (2015). Disruptive practices: Advancing social justice through feminist community-based service learning in higher education. In A. S. Tinkler, B. E., Tinkler, V. M. Jagla, & J. R. Strait (Eds.), *Service learning to advance social justice in a time of radical inequality* (pp. 65–94). Charlotte, NC: Information Age Publishing.

Diemer, M. A., Hsieh, C. A., & Pan, T. (2009). School and parental influences on sociopolitical development among poor adolescents of color. *The Counseling Psychologist*, *37*(2), 317–344.

Diemer, M. A., Kauffman, A., Koenig, N., Trahan, E., & Hsieh, C. A. (2006). Challenging racism, sexism, and social injustice: Support for urban adolescents' critical consciousness development. *Cultural Diversity and Ethnic Minority Psychology*, *12*(3), 444–460.

Diemer, M. A., & Li, C. H. (2011). Critical consciousness development and political participation among marginalized youth. *Child Development*, *82*(6), 1815–1833.

Diemer, M. A., & Rapa, L. J. (2016). Unraveling the complexity of critical consciousness, political efficacy, and political action among marginalized adolescents. *Child Development*, *87*(1), 221–238.

Diemer, M. A., Rapa, L. J., Park, C. J., & Perry, J. C. (2017). Development and validation of the critical consciousness scale. *Youth & Society, 49*(4), 461–483.

DuBois, D. L., Portillo, N., Rhodes, J. E., Silverthorn, N., & Valentine, J. C. (2011). How effective are mentoring programs for youth? A systematic assessment of the evidence. *Psychological Science in the Public Interest, 12*(2), 57–91.

Dunlap, M., Scoggin, J., Green, P., & Davi, A. (2007). White students' experiences of privilege and socioeconomic disparities: Toward a theoretical model. *Michigan Journal of Community Service Learning, 13*(2), 19–30.

Eyler, J., & Giles Jr, D. E. (1999). *Where's the learning in service-learning? Jossey-Bass Higher and Adult Education Series.* San Francisco, CA: Jossey-Bass, Inc.

Freire, P. (1970). *Pedagogy of the oppressed* (MB Ramos, Trans.). New York, NY: Continuum.

Freire, P. (1973). *Education for critical consciousness* (Vol. 1). London: Bloomsbury Publishing.

Freire, P. (1985). *The politics of education: Culture, power and liberation.* Westport, CT: Bergin & Garvey Publishers.

Freire, P., Fraser, J. W., Macedo, D., McKinnon, T., & Stokes, W. T. (1997). *Mentoring the mentor: A critical dialogue with Paulo Freire.* New York, NY: Peter Lang Publishing.

Garringer, M., McQuillen, S., & McDaniel, H. (2017). *Examining youth mentoring services across America: Findings from the 2016 National Mentoring Program Survey.* Boston, MA: MENTOR – The National Mentoring Partnership.

Godfrey, E. B., & Grayman, J. K. (2014). Teaching citizens: The role of open classroom climate in fostering critical consciousness among youth. *Journal of Youth and Adolescence, 43*(11), 1801–1817.

Green, A. E. (2001). "But you aren't white": Racial perceptions and service-learning. *Michigan Journal of Community Service Learning, 8*(1), 18.

Green, A. E. (2003). Difficult stories: Service-learning, race, class, and whiteness. *College Composition and Communication, 55*(2), 276–301.

Hall, H. R. (2015). Food for thought: Using critical pedagogy in mentoring African American adolescent males. *The Black Scholar, 45*(3), 39–53.

HM Treasury, Prime Minister's Office (2016, March 14). *PM announces new support to improve the life chances of millions* [Press Release]. Retrieved from https://www.gov.uk/government/news/pm-announces-new-support-to-improve-the-life-chances-of-millions

Hughes, C., Boyd, E., & Dykstra, S. J. (2010). Evaluation of a university-based mentoring program: Mentors' perspectives on a service-learning experience. *Mentoring & Tutoring: Partnership in Learning, 18*(4), 361–382.

Hughes, C., Steinhorn, R., Davis, B., Beckrest, S., Boyd, E., & Cashen, K. (2012). University-based service learning: Relating mentoring experiences to issues of poverty. *Journal of College Student Development, 53*(6), 767–782.

Hui, S. M. Y. (2009). Difficult dialogues about service learning: Embrace the messiness. *About Campus, 14*(5), 22–26.

Keys, C., McConnell, E, Motley, D., Liao, L., & McAuliff, K. (2017). The what, the how and the when of empowerment: Reflections on an intellectual history. In M. Bond, I. Serrano-García, &C. Keys (Eds.), *Handbook of community psychology.* Washington DC: American Psychological Association.

King, J. T. (2004). Service-learning as a site for critical pedagogy: A case of collaboration, caring, and defamiliarization across borders. *Journal of Experiential Education, 26*(3), 121–137.

Kirshner, B., & Ginwright, S. (2012). Youth organizing as a developmental context for African American and Latino adolescents. *Child Development Perspectives, 6*(3), 288–294.

Krauss, S. E., Collura, J., Zeldin, S., Ortega, A., Abdullah, H., & Sulaiman, A. H. (2014). Youth–adult partnership: Exploring contributions to empowerment, agency and community connections in Malaysian youth programs. *Journal of Youth and Adolescence, 43*(9), 1550–1562.

Liang, B., Spencer, R., West, J., & Rappaport, N. (2013). Expanding the reach of youth mentoring: Partnering with youth for personal growth and social change. *Journal of Adolescence, 36*(2), 257–267.

McIntosh, P. (1988). *White privilege: Unpacking the invisible knapsack.* Retrieved from https://www.racialequitytools.org/resourcefiles/mcintosh.pdf

Mitchell, T. D. (2007). Critical service-learning as social justice education: A case study of the citizen scholars program. *Equity & Excellence in Education, 40*(2), 101–112.

O'Donoghue, J. L., & Strobel, K. R. (2007). Directivity and freedom: Adult support of activism among urban youth. *American Behavioral Scientist, 51*(3), 465–485.

Okun, T. (2010). *The emperor has no clothes: Teaching about race and racism to people who don't want to know* (Doctoral dissertation). Retrieved from https://libres.uncg.edu/ir/uncg/f/okun_uncg_0154d_10299.pdf

Quiroz-Martínez, J., HoSang, D., & Villarosa, L. (2004). *Changing the rules of the game: Youth development & structural racism.* Washington, DC: Philanthropic Initiative for Racial Equity.

Rhodes, J. E. (2018, October 4). Mentoring youth in a divided nation [web blog]. Retrieved from https://www.evidencebasedmentoring.org/mentoring-youth-in-a-deeply-divided-nation/

Sánchez, B., & Colón, Y. (2005). Race, ethnicity, and culture in mentoring relationships. In D. L. Dubois & M. L. Karcher (Eds.), *Handbook of youth mentoring* (pp. 191–204). Thousand Oaks, CA: Sage.

Schwartz, S. E., & Rhodes, J. E. (2016). From treatment to empowerment: New approaches to youth mentoring. *American Journal of Community Psychology, 58*(1–2), 150–157.

Seider, S., Tamerat, J., Clark, S., & Soutter, M. (2017). Investigating adolescents' critical consciousness development through a character framework. *Journal of Youth and Adolescence, 46*(6), 1162–1178.

Shiller, J. T. (2013). Preparing for democracy: How community-based organizations build civic engagement among urban youth. *Urban Education, 48*(1), 69–91.

Valentino, S., & Wheeler, M. (2013). *Big Brothers Big Sisters report to America: Positive outcomes for a positive future. 2013 Youth Outcomes Report.* Retrieved from http://www.bbbs-gc.org/Websites/bbbsgallatincounty/images/20130425_BBBSA_YOS2013.pdf

Watts, R. J., Diemer, M. A., & Voight, A. M. (2011). Critical consciousness: Current status and future directions. *New Directions for Child and Adolescent Development, 2011*(134), 43–57.

Watts, R. J., & Flanagan, C. (2007). Pushing the envelope on youth civic engagement: A developmental and liberation psychology perspective. *Journal of Community Psychology, 35*(6), 779–792.

Weiston-Serdan, T. (2017). *Critical mentoring: A practical guide.* Sterling, VA: Stylus Publishing.

Zeldin, S., Christens, B. D., & Powers, J. L. (2013). The psychology and practice of youth-adult partnership: Bridging generations for youth development and community change. *American Journal of Community Psychology, 51*(3–4), 385–397.

Zeldin, S., Larson, R., Camino, L., & O'Connor, C. (2005). Intergenerational relationships and partnerships in community programs: Purpose, practice, and directions for research. *Journal of Community Psychology, 33*(1), 1–10.

Zimmerman, M. A. (1990). Taking aim on empowerment research: On the distinction between individual and psychological conceptions. *American Journal of Community Psychology, 18*(1), 169–177.

Zimmerman, M. A., Bingenheimer, J. B., & Behrendt, D. E. (2005). Natural mentoring relationships. In D. L. Dubois, & M. L. Karcher (Eds.), *Handbook of youth mentoring* (pp. 143–157). Thousand Oaks, CA: Sage.

Chapter 4

New approaches to empower youth to recruit mentors in the United States

Sarah Schwartz, McKenna Parnes, Laura Austin, and Rebecca Browne

Broadly speaking, youth mentoring is defined as a relationship between a young person and an older, more experienced, non-parental figure who provides them with support and guidance (DuBois & Karcher, 2005). Youth mentoring aims to promote positive developmental outcomes and youth well-being by providing youth with a caring relationship with an adult, which is thought to generalise to other relationships in the youth's life. Formal mentoring is one approach to youth mentoring in which youth are paired with volunteer adult mentors through a programme, as opposed to natural mentoring in which relationships develop organically between youth and adults within their networks. While formal mentoring programmes can result in long-lasting, supportive relationships with adults, too often formal mentoring matches end prematurely and do not have long-lasting effects (e.g. Aseltine et al., 2000; Grossman & Rhodes, 2002; Herrera, Grossman, Kaugh, & McMaken, 2011). Formal mentoring rests on the assumptions (1) that by matching a young person with a volunteer adult, a close and supportive relationship will develop between them and (2) that a positive mentoring relationship generalises to other relationships, improving a mentee's ability to effectively interact with other adults in their lives. Unfortunately, however, not all matched mentors and mentees connect and develop close relationships, and even when they do, some youth may require more explicit skills-based and scaffolded approaches to learn how to cultivate supportive relationships with adults. New approaches to youth mentoring seek to address these limitations by empowering youth to identify potential mentors and supportive adults from within their existing social networks.

This chapter will review the theory and research on new approaches to youth mentoring that centre on youth agency. First, we describe the literature on the traditional approach to youth mentoring – formal mentoring – and discuss its strengths and limitations as an intervention for youth connectedness and well-being. Then, using a developmental systems approach, we explore new approaches to youth mentoring that empower youth and emphasise the development of youth's individual skills and attitudes related to building connections with adults. Youth-Initiated Mentoring and Connected Scholars are highlighted as well as other promising approaches to that empower youth to recruit mentors and build systems of support. Finally, future directions for the field of mentoring are discussed.

Formal approaches to youth mentoring

To date, the majority of research and funding for youth mentoring has focused on formal mentoring programmes. Typically, formal mentoring programmes have focused their efforts on recruiting volunteer mentors to form one-on-one relationships with youth who have been identified as "at-risk", in hopes of improving their developmental outcomes. Youth mentoring programmes emerged from the Progressive Era in the United States and in the context of the widening class divide of the early 1900s. Growing concern over the increasing number of children being born into poverty led to the creation of a wide range of social service programmes for low income youth (Schwartz & Rhodes, 2016). The first formal mentoring programme to be born out of this era was Big Brothers Big Sisters of America (BBBSA). The programme, founded in 1904, served as an impetus for middle class Americans to serve as volunteers and provide support and guidance to low-income children. Currently, BBBSA is the largest formal mentoring programme in America and operates in 12 countries across the globe. Since the creation of BBBSA, countless other formal mentoring programmes have been developed and implemented with youth. More recently, formal mentoring is seeing growth in many countries around the world. New Zealand, Canada, Israel, Mexico, and the UK, to name a few, have well established youth mentoring programmes. Although the approach to youth mentoring has developed in many positive ways over the past century, many formal youth mentoring programmes still struggle to pull away from the individual-focused and deficit-based paradigm that historically characterised youth mentoring in the United States.

Unsurprisingly, there is substantial diversity among youth mentoring programmes in their structure and their goals. Mentoring programmes may be community- or school-based, as well as group or individual, and receive funding from individuals, communities, corporations, and/or governments. Some mentoring programmes choose to focus on promoting positive youth development in general, whereas others adopt more targeted goals relating to education and/or employment. Regardless of their specific focus, the goal of youth mentoring is to increase the number of young people who have at least one supportive relationship with a non-parental adult (Schwartz & Rhodes, 2016). Importantly, relationships with mentors are thought to generalise to other relationships in the mentee's life, thus empowering youth to interact with others more effectively. In particular, by providing caring support, mentors can both challenge negative views that some youth may hold of themselves and show that positive relationships with non-parental adults are possible (Rhodes, Schwartz, Willis, & Wu, 2017).

Youth mentoring programmes engage with a variety of volunteer mentors, many of whom have little or no formal training or experience in the helping fields. Considering this, there is a general agreement within the field that some type of orientation should be offered, and that mentors should receive on-going support (DuBois, Holloway, Valentine, & Cooper, 2002). After training has taken place, many programmes aim to match youth with mentors on the basis of criteria such as gender, race/ethnicity, or mutual interests when possible. Notably, matching youth based on gender and race/ethnicity is often not possible, as formal mentors are most often White middle-class women, while many programmes target low-income communities and communities of colour (DuBois et al., 2002). Regardless of how youth are matched with a mentor, there is little consistency in programme match length requirements and frequency of meetings across mentoring programmes, with some matches lasting a lifetime and others lasting only weeks or months.

Mentoring programmes have been widely studied over the past 20 years. However, research on their effectiveness has shown varying results (Rhodes & DuBois, 2008). A recent meta-analysis of U.S.-based evaluations assessing the impact of formal youth mentoring programmes (DuBois, Portillo, Rhodes, Silverthorn, & Valentine, 2011) has emphasised the potential for mentoring programmes to positively impact youth. In this meta-analysis, 73 samples from programme evaluations were coded on features including evaluation methodology (e.g. research design), programme features (e.g. specific goals), characteristics of youth (e.g. age), mentoring relationships (e.g. frequency of meeting), and type of outcome assessed (e.g. behavioural). Overall, findings suggest that mentoring programmes yield modest positive effects for youth (.21). Stronger programme effects were found to be associated with several factors: (a) programmes serving youth who have been involved in problem behaviours, (b) programmes serving a larger proportion of male youth, (c) programmes serving youth with greater levels of both individual and environmental risk, (d) a relatively strong fit between the educational/occupational backgrounds of mentors and the programme's goals, (e) the matching of youth and mentors based on similarity of interests, and (f) the youth not residing in single-parent households. Notably, the most prominent moderator was mentor-mentee similarity, highlighting the importance of taking match affinity and closeness into consideration.

Other research has shown the benefits resulting from youth mentoring largely depend on the length and quality of the relationships that are formed between mentors and youth (Rhodes et al., 2017). Moreover, research has demonstrated that the early termination of mentoring relationships may have a negative impact on youth (DuBois et al., 2002). Yet, some data indicates that as many as half of relationships in formal mentoring relationships end prematurely (Herrera et al., 2011). Research indicates that stronger and longer-lasting relationships develop when mentors adopt a flexible, youth-centred style, in which the young person's interests and preferences are underscored (Deutsch & Spencer, 2009).

These relatively modest effects discussed above may be explained by the current limitations of formal mentoring programmes. Most importantly, as evident from the high rates of premature termination, not all assigned mentoring relationships develop into a genuine and supportive relationship between a youth and an adult. Moreover, many mentoring programmes rely on the assumption that mentoring relationships are generalisable, and that through being matched with a volunteer mentor, youth will learn to interact with other adults more effectively. However, many programmes do not place a focus on building the skills necessary for youth to form subsequent relationships. Finally, by focusing solely on the relationship between a mentee and a volunteer mentor, youth mentoring decontextualises the young person and too often disregards the role of the community and other adults in the young person's life (Schwartz & Rhodes, 2016). Although, to date, the bulk of research and programming in youth mentoring has been devoted primarily to formal youth mentoring, there is growing attention on new approaches to mentoring that leverage natural mentoring relationships and empower young people to build connections with adults who can best support their interests and needs.

New approaches to empower youth to recruit mentors

A developmental systems approach can provide a useful frame to understand youth mentoring interventions. This approach aims to develop assets both within the youth (e.g. sense of purpose; interpersonal competence; academic engagement) and within the youth's environment (e.g. family support, non-parental adult relationships). Importantly, this theory emphasises fit between internal and external assets (Benson & Scales, 2009; Lerner et al., 2015). Bringing this frame to youth mentoring, it is important both to develop youth's individual skills and attitudes related to building connections with adults as well as increase the availability of adult mentors. Youth mentoring interventions have largely focused on the latter but have placed little emphasis on the former. We propose expanding our focus on youth mentoring to include not only programmes that match volunteer mentors with individual youth, but also those interventions that promote youth-adult connectedness more generally. By doing so, we make space for a range of approaches that aim to facilitate natural mentoring relationships and, in particular, those that empower youth to cultivate and draw on such connections. Below, we describe the current research on these new and innovative approaches to youth mentoring.

Youth-Initiated Mentoring

Youth-Initiated Mentoring (YIM) has growing recognition as an alternative model to traditional mentoring programmes in which youth nominate adults within their pre-existing social networks to serve as their mentors. Staff affiliated with a YIM programme then provide screening, training, and oversight to the chosen adult as a way to support the relationship. YIM combines the strengths of informal and formal mentoring strategies, such that this approach encourages youth to draw on mentors already available to them in their community while providing the mentoring relationship with scaffolding and structured support (Schwartz, Rhodes, Spencer, & Grossman, 2013). Thus, YIM can help foster mentoring relationships that are enduring while supporting youth to strengthen existing relationships and build social capital.

YIM addresses many of the challenges identified in formal and informal mentoring approaches. As noted earlier, in formal mentoring programmes, the majority of volunteers are White, middle class, women, resulting in many youth being matched with volunteers of different race, gender, and socio-economic backgrounds (e.g. Garringer, McQuillin, & McDaniel, 2017; Tierney, Grossman, & Resch, 2000). This mismatch in experience paired with a lack of prior relationship can lead to challenges in the mentoring relationship, especially with regard to issues of mentor retention and premature match closings (Greeson, 2013; Taussig & Weiler, 2017). A benefit of YIM is that youth are able to choose mentors who hold similar cultural, ethnic, and/or racial identities, or come from similar backgrounds, setting a strong foundation for the mentoring relationships. In fact, research indicates that mentors and mentees share the same racial or ethnic background in the majority (more than 80%) of YIM matches (Schwartz et al., 2013).

Additionally, in formal mentoring, volunteer mentors may enter the relationship with high expectations of bonding with youth, and then feel defeated when struggling to connect in the early stages of the relationship (Spencer, 2007). Such unrealistic expectations can result in volunteer dropout and match endings (e.g. Herrera, DuBois, & Grossman, 2013; Kupersmidt, Stump, Stelter, & Thodes, 2017; Spencer, Basualdo-Delmonico, Walsh, & Drew, 2017). Adults recruited through YIM who are already familiar with youth may have more tempered, realistic expectations of the relationship and may already have made it through the initial stages of relationship and trust-building (e.g. Spencer, Drew, Gowdy, & Horn, 2018; Spencer, Gowdy, Drew, & Rhodes, 2019). Furthermore, youth's initiative and vulnerability in choosing a mentor may demonstrate to adults that they are invested in the mentoring relationship, thus eliciting greater commitment and persistence in the relationship (e.g. Spencer et al., 2019). At the same time, YIM may also address a major drawback of informal mentoring, specifically, that not all youth have access to skills or resources to help them recruit informal mentors. By providing youth support in the process of identifying and recruiting mentors from their community, YIM may expand access to mentoring relationships.

YIM was first implemented in the National Guard Youth ChalleNGe Program (NGYCP), an intensive residential treatment programme aimed at re-engaging adolescents who dropped out of high school. This approach was instituted as an attempt to address erosion effects that occur in many residential programmes for higher risk youth (Bloom, 2010). An evaluation of YIM indicated this was an effective strategy for improving youth outcomes at a 3-year follow-up across educational and vocational contexts, and decreasing outcomes related to delinquent behaviour (Schwartz et al., 2013; Spencer, Tugenberg, Ocean, Schwartz, & Rhodes, 2016). Moreover, Schwartz et al. (2013) demonstrated that mentoring relationships were long-lasting when youth (rather than their parents or programme staff) took an active role in identifying adults to serve as mentors and when mentors and mentees shared the same racial or ethnic background. Overall, this initial research on YIM provides support for this approach as an effective way to promote both positive youth development and mentoring relationship development.

Given these promising findings, the research base on YIM has expanded to explore this approach in other contexts. One study examined whether Dutch adolescents with complex needs would benefit from the YIM approach as an alternative to out-of-home placement. Youth were either placed in the treatment group (YIM) or the control group (residential treatment). Findings revealed that the majority of youth in the treatment group were able to nominate a mentor and demonstrated that YIM could serve as an effective substitute for out-of-home placement (van Dam et al., 2017). YIM has also been assessed as a prevention strategy to support system-involved youth, both in the juvenile justice system and child welfare system, who are transitioning to independent living (Spencer et al., 2019). Spencer et al.'s (2019) qualitative study, drawing on youth, parent, and mentor perspectives, found that YIM may be a beneficial intervention to aide system-involved youth in recruiting supportive adult relationships. Youth nominated adults to serve as mentors with guidance from the mentoring programme and parents and intentionally sought out mentors whom they believed were trustworthy and non-judgemental (e.g. teachers, previous caseworkers, extended family members). The majority of mentors reported they agreed to serve in this role because the specific youth had requested their support, though many had to carefully consider whether their schedules or work policies would allow them to take on the commitment and remain dedicated (Spencer et al., 2019). Importantly, this research suggests that YIM may reach a pool of mentors that formal mentoring programmes rarely access. Mentor and youth perspectives also indicated that allowing youth autonomy in choosing their own mentors can facilitate strong and meaningful relationships that promote psychological and social well-being and future orientation among system-involved youth (Spencer et al., 2019).

Taken together, the research speaks to the promise of YIM as an intervention to provide higher risk youth with supportive mentoring relationships. YIM relationships appear to be enduring (e.g. Schwartz et al., 2013), may serve as alternatives to out-home-placement for youth (van Dam et al., 2017), and address limitations of more traditional mentoring approaches, such as mentor retention and premature match endings (Greeson, 2013; Taussig & Weiler, 2017). Additionally, the programmatic support provided through YIM to formalise pre-existing ties helps youth who may not yet possess skills to independently identify and recruit informal mentors. Despite its promise, however, research on YIM is still emerging and would benefit from more rigorous studies that randomly assign youth to either receive YIM or traditional mentoring, which would allow for causal conclusions to be drawn regarding the efficacy of YIM. There is also a need for further research on best practices in YIM programming as well as potential for negative effects, for example if mentors chosen by youth refuse to take on the role or if relationships end prematurely.

Connected scholars: teaching students to recruit mentors and build social capital

Building on the model of youth recruiting their own mentors, Connected Scholars is a programme designed to empower adolescents and young adults – specifically targeting first-generation college students – to build connections and identify mentors who can help them advance their academic and career goals (Schwartz et al., 2016). Research and theory highlight the importance of having access to supportive networks for college student well-being (Kuh, Kinzie, Buckley, Bridges, & Hayek, 2006). Social capital – an individual's social network that can provide access to information, resources, or support (Coleman, 1990) – is particularly important for first year college students' (Brouwer, Jansen, Flache, & Hofman, 2016) and underrepresented college students' (Hurd, Albright, Wittrup, Negrete, & Billingsley, 2018; Strayhorn, 2010) adjustment and academic achievement. During this period of transition, social capital can help students connect with institutional agents (e.g. campus faculty and staff) who are able to provide information about additional resources and services offered that may facilitate academic and career opportunities (Burt, 2005; Stanton-Salazar, 2011). Connections with faculty have been shown to contribute to students' academic success (Baker, 2013), engagement (Umbach & Wawrynznski, 2005), and sense of academic and social integration (Deil-Amen, 2011). These relationships may evolve into mentoring relationships focused on fostering growth and achievement through role modelling, support, and advocacy (Crisp & Cruz, 2009).

While access to support is associated with students' academic success and may help students take better advantage of their college experience, not all students have equal access to or understanding of support services offered

(Sarason, Sarason, & Pierce, 1990; York-Anderson & Bowman, 1991). For example, Karp, O'Gara, and Hughes (2008) found that while campuses offer support services that are open to all students, those who take advantage of these resources are often those who have already social and cultural resources that existed prior to attending college. Furthermore, students with lower levels of social and cultural capital found it difficult to access services even when colleges tried to provide students with structured opportunities to partake in to promote social integration (Karp et al., 2008).

Differences in students' attitudes towards help-seeking (i.e. avoidance or intention to seek help [Karabenick, 2003]) and network orientation (i.e. one's perceptions about the benefits of support resources [Vaux, Burda, & Stewart, 1986]) may contribute to disparities in access to support (Smith & Blacknall, 2010). Often students who need the most help avoid it because they do not want to publicly draw attention to their academic challenges and confirm negative beliefs about their inability to be successful in academic settings (Ames & Lau, 1982). In contrast, the more students perceive themselves as being academically capable, socially competent, and connected to their college, the more likely they will be to seek help (Karabenick, 2003). Moreover, some students face greater challenges related to belonging and engagement on college campuses due to their identities and backgrounds. Specifically, first-generation college students, compared to their continuing generation peers, show lower levels of campus engagement (Chen, 2005), and are less likely to use campus support services (Terenzini, Springer, Yaeger, Pascarella, & Nora, 1996) or seek help during college (Jenkins, Miyazaki, & Janosik, 2009).

In the context of an interactive course, Connected Scholars helps students learn how to cultivate networks of support and provides students with a space to practice strategies for recruiting and maintaining relationships with mentors. This programme was created to address limitations of current approaches to support students. While many college institutions assign all students a formal academic advisor, studies have shown low student satisfaction with these advisors (Allard & Parashar, 2013). A major problem with formally matching students with mentors is that many students with the highest needs are the least likely to use these services (Alexitch, 2002), possibly because these programmes rely on skills for engaging with adults in a college setting that students – especially first-generation college students – have not yet cultivated (Lareau & Cox, 2011). The goal of Connected Scholars is to support students in developing these skills and attitudes that will help them continue to foster mentoring relationships throughout their lives.

Connected Scholars is delivered through a series of group-based lessons including main components of: (1) offering instruction and discussing the role of social capital in goal attainment; (2) facilitating activities that will help students identify available connections and potential ones for the future; and (3) engaging in experiential activities and real-world practice of reaching out to potential mentors and cultivating relationships with faculty and staff. Topics and activities include: discussing the importance of mentors, social capital, and personal goals; identifying a personal brand; highlighting strategies for developing and maintaining mentoring relationships (e.g. attending office hours, emailing, scheduling, writing thank you notes); navigating the challenges of networking (e.g. managing potential rejection); creating a visual representation of all current and potential sources of support (i.e. eco-mapping); practicing skills for reaching out to and strengthening relationships with mentors through role-playing activities and interviews with potential mentors; and attending a networking event with identified mentors.

Research on the effectiveness of Connected Scholars demonstrates this may be a promising approach for cultivating help-seeking and networking skills in both high school and college students. An exploratory investigation of Connected Scholars was initially conducted with twelve ethnic minority, low-income, and first-generation college-bound high school seniors. The programme was offered as an eight-session workshop and data was drawn from pre- and post-intervention semi-structured interviews with all participants, research observations in the classroom, and participant feedback and workshop materials. Results of the pilot study demonstrated that Connected Scholars increased the value students placed on social capital and mentoring relationships, and developed students' skills, knowledge, and self-efficacy in pursuing such connections (Schwartz et al., 2016).

The qualitative pilot study was followed by a mixed-methods quasi-experimental study investigating the impact of Connected Scholars on incoming students in a summer remedial programme at a public, urban, commuter-campus college in the Northeast. Participants in this study included a subsample of first-generation college students who either attended the summer programme in 2014 or 2015. Baseline data was collected for both cohorts in June prior to the programme start. Students from the 2014 cohort received treatment-as-usual (TAU) academic programming, and students in the 2015 cohort received TAU academic programming plus 4 hours of the Connected Scholars intervention. The program included 6 weeks of academic programming, meeting 4 days per week, and due to programme time constraints the original eight-session intervention was cut down to four weekly 1-hour sessions. Follow-up data was collected during the last week of the programme for students in both the treatment and comparison group, and at the end of students' first year of college, university records were obtained including grade point average (GPA). Results of this study indicated that compared to students who participated in TAU programming, students receiving Connected Scholars showed strengthened beliefs about the importance of social capital, increased self-reported likelihood to seek support, improved relationships with instructors, and increased GPA in their first year of college (Schwartz et al., 2017).

Given the benefits of Connected Scholars for first-generation college students, a follow-up investigation drawing on the quantitative data of the full sample (first-generation and continuing-generation students) from the aforementioned study was conducted to understand the mechanisms of change underlying the Connected Scholars intervention. Specifically, the study sought to examine student help-seeking attitudes and network orientation as potential mediators of the relationship between participation in the Connected Scholars intervention and student outcomes (i.e. relationships with instructors and GPA), and investigated differential impacts of Connected Scholars for first-generation students versus continuing-generation students. Findings from this study demonstrated that changes in students' help-seeking attitudes accounted for the impact of Connected Scholars intervention on students' GPA, while changes in students' network orientation related to their past help-seeking experiences accounted for the impact of Connected Scholars on students' relationships with instructors. Moreover, the indirect effect of the Connected Scholars intervention on student outcomes through changes in students' help-seeking attitudes and network orientation was observed only for first-generation students (Parnes, Kanchewa, Marks, & Schwartz, 2020).

Findings from these studies suggest that Connected Scholars is an effective approach to facilitate the development of positive help-seeking attitudes and network orientation among underrepresented students. Not only does participation in Connected Scholars empower youth to cultivate networks of support, it also has a positive direct and indirect impact on students' academic performance and relationships with instructors. Given that the research on Connected Scholars has only been examined within the context of a quasi-experimental study design, there is a need for more rigorous research evaluating the intervention's effects as well as research examining the intervention across different populations. Additionally, Connected Scholars was designed specifically for college students, but it is likely that workshops teaching young people how to recruit mentors and build social capital could be relevant in a range of other youth-serving settings. It will be important for future research to examine this potential.

Other promising approaches to facilitating natural mentoring relationships

Youth-Initiated Mentoring (YIM) and Connected Scholars are only two of many other possible strategies to support youth in forming supportive mentoring relationships with adults. For too long, research and practice have focused primarily on formal mentoring interventions. Although there is currently very limited research on other approaches, below we highlight three promising strategies.

Project DREAM is an intervention in which middle school students are supported in identifying and recruiting a positive adult from their existing social network who, after being screened, participates with them in an afterschool programme (Hurd & Deutsch, 2015). The programme includes 8 weekly sessions focusing on a range of topics related to social-emotional learning such as personal strengths, goal-setting, and communicating with and soliciting support from adults. The programme aims to facilitate the development of natural mentoring relationships among young adolescents who otherwise might not have such relationships. More broadly, the goal of the programme is to empower youth to identify caring adults in their community and to "socialize youth and adult participants toward relationships where youth are empowered to lead and adults are encouraged to play a strong supportive role" (Albright, Hurd, & Hussain, 2017, p. 14). Although there is not yet research addressing the extent to which the programme achieves these goals, this programme represents an innovative example of how programmes can honour youth choice, acknowledge the positive adults within youth's communities, and facilitate natural mentoring relationships in a safe, supportive context. This is particularly important since adults are often less willing to make space for such approaches among younger adolescents.

While the approaches described thus far focus on empowering youth to identify and recruit mentors, the goal of *Caregiver Initiated Mentoring* is to empower parents and caregivers to recruit mentors to support their younger children (Weiler, Kazlauskaite, Keyzers, & Cavell, 2018). In recognition of the fact that it may not be developmentally appropriate for younger children to initiate mentoring relationships with adults, and that too often, caregivers' knowledge, experiences, and preferences are not taken into account in traditional approaches to mentoring, Caregiver Initiated Mentoring would support caregivers in connecting their children with other positive adults. Although this model is still being developed, it holds significant potential for facilitating informal mentoring relationships for children as well as for building parents' "village" of support in the process of raising children. At the same time, initial focus groups with caregivers indicate a number of barriers to overcome, including not wanting to ask for help, safety concerns, and lacking connections to the types of role models they wanted for their children (Weiler et al., 2018). Interestingly, most caregivers reported feeling more comfortable with mentors in the context of formal mentoring programmes than with informal mentors. These findings highlight the challenges inherent in the creation of new models of mentoring that are less familiar than traditional formal mentoring models and the importance of carefully developing such interventions with the input of families, including both caregivers and youth.

A final strategy that should be part of any attempt to increase natural mentoring relationships is *Everyday Mentoring* or *Intentional Mentoring*. The goal of this approach is to increase the quantity and quality of potential informal mentors. To use a well-known metaphor, while earlier strategies described focus primarily on "teaching youth (or caregivers) to fish," this approach focuses on "stocking the pond." Everyday Mentoring aims to provide training and/or web-based resources around best practices in mentoring to any interested adults who interact with youth, be they afterschool providers, coaches, or caring adults in the community (see: https://everydaymentor.org/; http://www.mentoringpittsburgh.org/pages/everyday-mentoring). These approaches may be particularly important alongside strategies encouraging youth to reach out to adults in their existing social network to increase the likelihood that willing and able informal mentors are available. A related approach focuses on the importance of these adults, also intentionally connecting youth to other supportive adults and experiences. In a paper entitled, "Not just a blip in someone's life: integrating brokering practices into out-of-school programming as a means of supporting and expanding youth futures," authors Ching, Santo, Hoadley, and Peppler (2016) discuss how adults working with youth can prioritise not only developing caring connections with the youth they serve, but also to function as "brokers" who connect youth to other supportive adults, programmes, or institutions.

As stated earlier, these are only a few examples of possible approaches to facilitating natural mentoring relationships and, more generally, caring connections between adults and young people. It also should be noted that these approaches are not mutually exclusive with more traditional formal mentoring programmes. In fact, few formal mentoring programmes are designed to create relationships that will last indefinitely. More often, mentoring programme aim for a youth and an adult to meet regularly for a limited amount of time, typically 1 year, with the hope that the experience of connecting with a caring adult will generalise to the youth's other relationships (Rhodes, Spencer, Keller, Liang, & Noam, 2006). Encouragingly, research suggests that close formal mentoring relationships are associated with improvements in relationships with parents and teachers (Chan et al., 2013; DuBois, Nevill, Parra, & Pugh-Lilly, 2002; Karcher, Davis, & Powell, 2002; Rhodes, Reddy, & Grossman, 2005). It is possible, however, that more intentional approaches to building youth's capacity to identify and reach out to other supportive adults in the context of a formal mentoring relationship could better equip youth to connect with natural mentors even after their formal relationship has ended. Recent research indicates that when mentors engage in more active strategies to connect their mentees to other adults, youth demonstrate improved outcomes related to connectedness and help-seeking (Austin, Herrera, Jarjoura, & Schwartz, 2019). By incorporating strategies to facilitate natural mentoring relationships into mentor training or as part of programme termination rituals, formal mentoring programmes may be able to demonstrate more enduring impacts by empowering youth to recruit mentors and other supportive connections throughout their lives.

Conclusion

Although formal youth mentoring programmes aim to foster positive youth development through the cultivation of a supportive mentoring relationship, such programmes are limited by premature relationship terminations, small effect sizes, and erosion of effects after the mentoring relationship ends (e.g. Aseltine et al., 2000; Grossman & Rhodes, 2002; Herrera et al., 2011). In response to these limitations of formal mentoring programmes, new approaches to youth mentoring seek to empower youth to identify potential mentors and supportive adults from within their existing social networks, combining the strengths of both formal and informal mentoring strategies. Bringing a developmental systems approach to youth mentoring, it is important to develop youth's individual skills and attitudes related to connecting with adults, as well as increasing the availability of adult mentors. While traditional approaches to youth mentoring focus primarily on the availability of adult mentors by introducing a single new adult into a young person's life, recent, innovative approaches incorporate skill building in order to promote natural mentoring relationships and youth–adult connectedness more generally.

In this chapter, YIM was highlighted as a new, empowering approach to youth mentoring, in which youth nominate adults within their pre-existing social networks to serve as their mentors. These organically selected mentoring relationships are then supported by a YIM programme, an approach that pulls from the strengths of both formal and informal mentoring (Schwartz et al., 2013). YIM has been used in a variety of contexts with youth that programmes historically have struggled to effectively serve, including adolescents who dropped out of high school and youth involved in the child welfare or juvenile justice system, with encouraging results.

Next, Connected Scholars was discussed as a related approach to empower adolescents and young adults to build connections and identify mentors who can help them advance their academic and career goals (Schwartz, Kanchewa, Rhodes, Cutler, & Cunningham, 2016). The interactive course helps students, and particularly first-generation college students, learn how to cultivate networks of support and provides a space for students to practice strategies for recruiting and maintaining relationships with mentors. Preliminary research on Connected Scholars suggests that it may be a promising approach for cultivating help-seeking and networking skills in both high school and college students.

The chapter concluded by discussing several other promising strategies to support youth in forming supportive mentoring relationships with adults: Project DREAM, Caregiver Initiated Mentoring, and Everyday Mentoring or Intentional Mentoring. Importantly, the chapter emphasises that formal mentoring and these new approaches are not mutually exclusive. Rather, by incorporating strategies to facilitate natural mentoring relationships, formal mentoring programmes may be able to strengthen and prolong their positive impacts by empowering youth to recruit mentors and supportive connections throughout their life.

References

Albright, J. N., Hurd, N. M., & Hussain, S. B. (2017). Applying a social justice lens to youth mentoring: A review of the literature and recommendations for practice. *American Journal of Community Psychology, 59*(3–4), 363–381.

Alexitch, L. R. (2002). The role of help-seeking attitudes and tendencies in students' preferences for academic advising. *Journal of College Student Development, 43*(1), 5–19.

Allard, F., & Parashar, S. (2013). Comparing undergraduate satisfaction with faculty and professional advisers: A multi-method approach. *The Mentor: An Academic Advising Journal.* Retrieved from https://journals.psu.edu/mentor/article/view/61283

Ames, R., & Lau, S. (1982). An attributional analysis of student help-seeking in academic settings. *Journal of Educational Psychology, 74*(3), 414–423.

Aseltine, R. H., Dupre, M., & Lamlein, P. (2000). Mentoring as a drug prevention strategy: An evaluation of across ages. *Adolescent and Family Health, 1*(1), 11–20.

Austin, L., Herrera, C., Jarjoura, R., Schwartz, S. (May, 2019). *Mentors Who Connect: The Impact of Mentoring Connecting Behaviors on Youth Relational Outcomes.* Poster presented at the Annual Meeting of the Society for Prevention Research, San Francisco, CA.

Baker, J. D. (2013). Social networking and professional boundaries. *AORN Journal, 97*(5), 501–506.

Benson, P. L., & C. Scales, P. (2009). The definition and preliminary measurement of thriving in adolescence. *The Journal of Positive Psychology, 4*(1), 85–104.

Bloom, D. (2010). Programs and policies to assist high school dropouts in the transition to adulthood. *The Future of Children, 20,* 89–108.

Brouwer, J., Jansen, E., Flache, A., & Hofman, W. (2016). The impact of social capital on self-efficacy and study success among first-year university students. *Learning and Individual Differences, 52,* 109–118.

Burt, R. S. (2005). *Brokerage and closure: An introduction to social capital.* Oxford: Oxford University Press.

Chan, C. S., Rhodes, J. E., Howard, W. J., Lowe, S. R., Schwartz, S. E., & Herrera, C. (2013). Pathways of influence in school-based mentoring: The mediating role of parent and teacher relationships. *Journal of School Psychology, 51*(1), 129–142.

Chen, X. (2005). First-generation students in postsecondary education: A look at their college transcripts. Retrieved from https://nces.ed.gov/pubs2005/2005171.pdf

Ching, D., Santo, R., Hoadley, C., & Peppler, K. (2016). Not just a blip in someone's life: Integrating brokering practices into out-of-school programming as a means of supporting and expanding youth futures. *On the Horizon, 24*(3), 296–312.

Coleman, James. (1990). *Foundations of social theory.* Cambridge, MA: Harvard University Press.

Crisp, G., & Cruz, I. (2009). Mentoring college students: A critical review of the literature between 1990 and 2007. *Research in Higher Education, 50,* 525–545.

Deil-Amen, R. (2011). The "traditional" college student: A smaller and smaller minority and its implications for diversity and access institutions. In *Mapping Broad-Access Higher Education Conference at Stanford University.* Accessed April, 1, p. 2014.

Deutsch, N. L., & Spencer, R. (2009). Capturing the magic: Assessing the quality of youth mentoring relationships. *New Directions for Youth Development, 2009*(121), 47–70.

DuBois, D. L., Holloway, B. E., Valentine, J. C., & Cooper, H. (2002). Effectiveness of mentoring programs for youth: A meta-analytic review. *American Journal of Community Psychology, 30*(2), 157–197.

DuBois, D. L., & Karcher, M. J. (2005). Youth mentoring. *Handbook of Youth Mentoring, 2*(11).

DuBois, D. L., Neville, H. A., Parra, G. R., & Pugh-Lilly, A. O. (2002). Testing a new model of mentoring. *New Directions for Youth Development, 2002*(93), 21–57.

DuBois, D. L., Portillo, N., Rhodes, J. E., Silverthorn, N., & Valentine, J. C. (2011). How effective are mentoring programs for youth? A systematic assessment of the evidence. *Psychological Science in the Public Interest, 12*(2), 57–91.

Garringer, M., McQuillin, S., & McDaniel, H. (2017). Examining youth mentoring services across America: Findings from the 2016 Mentoring Program Survey. Retrieved from https://www.mentoring.org/new-site/wp-content/uploads/2017/07/Mentor-Survey-Report_FINAL_small.pdf

Greeson, J. K. (2013). Foster youth and the transition to adulthood: The theoretical and conceptual basis for natural mentoring. *Emerging Adulthood, 1*(1), 40–51.

Grossman, J. B., & Rhodes, J. E. (2002). The test of time: Predictors and effects of duration in youth mentoring relationships. *American Journal of Community Psychology, 30*(2), 199–219.

Herrera, C., DuBois, D. L., & Grossman, J. B. (2013). The Role of Risk: Mentoring Experiences and Outcomes for Youth with Varying Risk Profiles. *MDRC*. Retrieved from https://www.mdrc.org/sites/default/files/Role%20of%20Risk_Final-web%20PDF.pdf

Herrera, C., Grossman, J. B., Kauh, T. J., & McMaken, J. (2011). Mentoring in schools: An impact study of Big Brothers Big Sisters school-based mentoring. *Child Development, 82*(1), 346–361.

Hurd, N. M., Albright, J., Wittrup, A., Negrete, A., & Billingsley, J. (2018). Appraisal support from natural mentors, self-worth, and psychological distress: Examining the experiences of underrepresented students transitioning through college. *Journal of Youth and Adolescence, 47*(5), 1100–1112.

Hurd, N. M., & Deutsch, N. L. (2015). *Development of Project DREAM: An after-school program to promote academic success via social and emotional learning and connectedness with adults*. Grant # R305A150028 funded through the Institute of Education Sciences. Available from: https://ies.ed.gov/funding/grantsearch/details.asp?ID=1724 [last accessed June 21 2019].

Jenkins, A. L., Miyazaki, Y., & Janosik, S. M. (2009). Predictors that distinguish first-generation college students from non-first generation college students. *Journal of Multicultural, Gender, and Minority Studies, 3*(1), 673–685.

Karabenick, S. A. (2003). Seeking help in large college classes: A person-centered approach. *Contemporary Educational Psychology, 28*(1), 37–58.

Karcher, M. J., Davis, C. III, & Powell, B. (2002). The effects of developmental mentoring on connectedness and academic achievement. *The School Community Journal, 12*(2), 35–50.

Karp, M. M., O'Gara, L., & Hughes, K. L. (2008). Do Support Services at Community Colleges Encourage Success or Reproduce Disadvantage? An Exploratory Study of Students in Two Community Colleges. CCRC Working Paper No. 10. *Community College Research Center, Columbia University*.

Kuh, G. D., Kinzie, J. L., Buckley, J. A., Bridges, B. K., & Hayek, J. C. (2006). *What matters to student success: A review of the literature* (Vol. 8). Washington, DC: National Postsecondary Education Cooperative.

Kupersmidt, J., Stump, K., Stelter, R., & Rhodes, J. (2017). Predictors of premature match closure in youth mentoring relationships. *American Journal of Community Psychology, 59*, 25–35.

Lareau, A., & Cox, C. (2011). Social class and the transition to adulthood: Differences in parents' interactions with institutions. In M. J. Carlson, & P. England (Eds.), *Social class and changing families in an unequal America*. Stanford, CA: Stanford University Press.

Lerner, R. M. (2015). Promoting positive human development and social justice: Integrating theory, research and application in contemporary developmental science. *International Journal of Psychology, 50*(3), 165–173.

Parnes, M. F., Kanchewa, S., Marks, A. K., & Schwartz, S. E. O. (2020). Closing the college achievement gap: Impacts and processes of a help-seeking intervention. *Journal of Applied Developmental Psychology*. 67. https://doi.org/10.1016/j.appdev.2020.101121

Rhodes, J. E. (Ed.). (2002). *New directions for youth development: Theory, practice, and research: A critical view of youth mentoring*. San Francisco: Jossey-Bass. (Gil Noam, series editor).

Rhodes, J. E. & DuBois, D. L. (2008). Mentoring relationships and programs for youth. *Current Directions in Psychological Science, 17*(4), 254–258.

Rhodes, J. E., Reddy, R., Roffman, J., & Grossman, J. B. (2005). Promoting successful youth mentoring relationships: A preliminary screening questionnaire. *Journal of Primary Prevention, 26*(2), 147–167.

Rhodes, J. E., Schwartz, S. E. O., Willis, M. M., & Wu, M. V. (2017). Validating a mentoring relationship quality scale: Does match strength predict match length? *Youth & Society, 49*(4) 415–437.

Rhodes, J. E., Spencer, R., Keller, T. E., Liang, B. & Noam, G. (2006). A model for the influence of mentoring relationships on youth development. *Journal of Community Psychology, 34*(6), 691–707.

Sarason, B. R., Sarason, I. G., & Pierce, G. R. (1990). *Social support: An interactional view*. John Wiley & Sons.

Schwartz, S. E. O., Chan, C. S., Rhodes, J., & Scales, P. C. (2013). Community developmental assets and positive youth development: The role of natural mentors. *Research in Human Development, 10*(2), 141–162.

Schwartz, S. E. O., Kanchewa, S. S., Rhodes, J. E., Cutler, E., & Cunningham, J. L. (2016). "I didn't know you could just ask:" Empowering underrepresented college-bound students to recruit academic and career mentors. *Children and Youth Services Review, 64*, 51–59.

Schwartz, S. E. O., Kanchewa, S., Spencer, R., Parnes, M., & Rhodes, J. E. (2017). I'm having a little struggle with this, can you help me out?" Examining impacts and processes of a social capital intervention for first-generation college students. *American Journal of Community Psychology*, 1–13.

Schwartz, S. E. O., & Rhodes, J. E. (2016). From treatment to empowerment: New approaches to youth mentoring. *American Journal of Community Psychology, 58*(1–2), 150–157.

Schwartz, S. E. O., Rhodes, J. E., Spencer, R., & Grossman, J. B. (2013). Youth initiated mentoring: Investigating a new approach to working with vulnerable adolescents. *American Journal of Community Psychology, 52*(1–2), 155–169.

Smith, E., & Blacknall, T. (2010). The Role of Social Supports and Self-Efficacy in College Success. *Research to Practice Brief. Pathways to College Network*. Retrieved from http://www.ihep.org/

Spencer, R. (2007). "It's not what I expected" A qualitative study of youth mentoring relationship failures. *Journal of Adolescent Research, 22*(4), 331–354.

Spencer, R., Gowdy, G., Drew, A. L., & Rhodes, J. E. (2019). "Who knows me the best and can encourage me the most?": Matching and early relationship development in youth-initiated mentoring relationships with system-involved youth. *Journal of Adolescent Research, 34*(1), 3–29.

Spencer, R., Tugenberg, T., Ocean, M., Schwartz, S. E. O., & Rhodes, J. E. (2016). "Somebody who was on my side" A qualitative examination of youth initiated mentoring. *Youth & Society, 48*(3), 402–424.

Stanton-Salazar, R. D. (2011). A social capital framework for the study of institutional agents and their role in the empowerment of low-status students and youth. *Youth & Society, 43*(3), 1066–1109.

Strayhorn, T. L. (2010). The influence of diversity on learning outcomes among African American college students: Measuring sex differences. *Journal of Student Affairs Research and Practice, 47*(3), 343–366.

Taussig, H., & Weiler, L. (2017). Mentoring for Youth in Foster Care. *National Mentoring Resource Center*. Retrieved from http://nationalmentoringresourcecenter.org/

Terenzini, P. T., Springer, L., Yaeger, P. M., Pascarella, E. T., & Nora, A. (1996). First-generation college students: Characteristics, experiences, and cognitive development. *Research in Higher Education, 37*(1), 1–22.

Tierney, J. P., Grossman, J. B., & Resch, N. L. (2000). Making a difference: An impact study of Big Brothers Big Sisters. *Public/Private Venture*. Retrieved from http://www.issuelab.org/

Umbach, P. D., & Wawrzynski, M. R. (2005). Faculty do matter: The role of college faculty in student learning and engagement. *Research in Higher Education, 46*(2), 153–184.

van Dam, L., Neels, S., de Winter, M., Branje, S., Wijsbroek, S., Hutschemaekers, G., … Stams, G. J. (2017). Youth initiated mentors: Do they offer an alternative for out-of-home placement in youth care? *British Journal of Social Work, 47*(6), 1764–1780.

van Dam, L., Smit, D., Wildschut, B., Branje, S. J. T., Rhodes, J. E., Assink, M., … Stams, G. J. J. (2018). Does natural mentoring matter? A multilevel meta-analysis on the association between natural mentoring and youth outcomes. *American Journal of Community Psychology, 62*(1–2), 203–220.

Vaux, A., Burda, P., & Stewart, D. (1986). Orientation toward utilization of support resources. *Journal of Community Psychology, 14*, 159–170.

Weiler, L., Kazlauskaite, V., Keyzers, A., & Cavell, T. (April, 2018). *Caregivers Fostering Mentoring Relationships for Positive Youth Development*. Paper presented at the Biennial Meeting of the Society for Research on Adolescence, Minneapolis, MN.

York-Anderson, D. C., & Bowman, S. L. (1991). Assessing the college knowledge of first-generation and second-generation college students. *Journal of College Student Development, 32*(2), 116–122.

Chapter 5

Youth-Initiated Mentoring

Promoting and improving the social networks of youth with complex needs in the Netherlands

Levi van Dam, Ellis ter Beek, and Natasha Koper

Professional care for juveniles with complex needs often lacks continuity (Konijn et al., 2019; Naert, Roose, Rapp, & Vanderplasschen, 2017; Souverein, Van der Helm, & Stams, 2013). Research suggests that at least one person should provide continuity for these juveniles and help them to express their needs (Pehlivan & Brummelman, 2015). Given the instability that youth with complex needs experience in their own family – due to disturbed relationships – the search for "arenas of comfort" is urgent, particularly during adolescence. An arena of comfort is a soothing and accepting context or a supportive relationship that gives the juvenile the chance to relax and rejuvenate, so that potentially stressful experiences and changes in another arena can be endured or mastered.

Although much research has focused on the role of parents in the development of children and adolescents, the role of other community adults, including family friends, neighbours, and teachers, has only recently been recognised as playing a vital role in the well-being of young people (Bowers, Johnson, Warren, Tirrell, & Lerner, 2015; Kesselring, De Winter, Van Yperen, & Lecluijze, 2016). Studies suggest that approximately three-quarters of adolescents have natural mentors within their social networks (Erickson, McDonald, & Elder, 2009; Raposa, Dietz, & Rhodes, 2017). A natural mentor is the result of an organically developing relationship between an adolescent and an older or more experienced individual who provides guidance and support over time. In contrast, formal mentoring programmes, in which a volunteer is matched with a young person, reach an estimated 7% of youth (Erickson et al., 2009; Raposa et al., 2017).

A recent meta-analysis of the effect of formal mentoring programmes on positive youth outcomes showed a small overall average effect size of $d = 0.19$ (Raposa et al., 2019). Similarly, a recent meta-analytic study on natural mentoring relationships showed that the mere *presence* of a natural mentor was associated with positive youth outcomes, with a small overall average effect size of Cohen's $d = .21$ (Van Dam et al., 2018). The association between the *quality* of the natural mentoring relationship (relatedness, social support and autonomy support) and positive youth outcomes yielded a medium overall average effect size ($d = .43$), with the largest effect sizes for social-emotional development ($d = .55$), and academic and vocational functioning ($d = .40$), and a small effect size ($d = .20$) for psychosocial problems. Notably, at-risk status (for instance, teenage mothers, homeless youth, youth in foster care and children of alcoholic parents) did not moderate the relation between presence and quality of natural mentoring relationships on the one hand and youth outcomes on the other hand, which is a positive finding for adolescents with complex needs.

Therefore, it seems appropriate to focus more on the social networks of youth with complex needs. How can youth benefit from existing supportive relationships, and how can professional care increase the value from this (untapped) resource? In this chapter, we describe the Youth-Initiated Mentoring (YIM) approach as it is developed in the Netherlands. First, we describe the motivation to develop a new approach, after which we explain this approach in more detail. Throughout our explanation, we clarify the approach in a more tangible way by describing several experiences from youth, parents, YIMs and professionals. We describe the first phase, in which the youth is invited to select a mentor from within his community, with practical explanations for professionals who want to adopt this new approach. We conclude this part with our "rules of thumb", which is a description of all the steps professionals should take into consideration if they want to work with this approach. We end this chapter with an overview of the extant research on this approach, and suggestions for future research.

Our motivation to develop the YIM approach

Many youth services work on continuity and client participation through organisational solutions, such as working with a case manager or a treatment trajectory coach. We focus on strengthening the juvenile's network through collaboration with an informal mentor, a YIM. This informal mentor is a person (e.g. relative, neighbour, or friend) adolescents nominate from their own social network, and who functions as a confidant and spokesman for the adolescent and a cooperation partner for parents and professionals (Schwartz et al., 2013; Spencer, Tugenberg, Ocean, Schwartz, & Rhodes, 2016). This fits with the international tendency in child and family social work to make use of the strengths of families and their own networks, and to stimulate client participation (Burford, 2005). The goal is to reduce psychological and behavioural problems of youth and his or her family, and to increase resilience through collaboration with the family and the wider social network.

Social networks are defined by the connections among the network members and transferal, that is, what is distributed through the existing connections (Christakis & Fowler, 2013). Professional involvement expands the existing network by adding new connections, and influences transferal by distributing new information. However, this expansion is temporary and its influence is often limited (Euser, Alink, Stoltenborgh, bakermans-kranenburg, & van IJzendoorn, 2015; Weisz et al., 2013), which is especially the case during out-of-home placement: there is a lack of continuity and trustworthy relationships due to placement instability (Strijker, Knorth, & Knot-Dickscheit, 2008). Also, the negative consequences of the instability of foster care placements have been highlighted in a vast body of research (Rock, Michelson, Thomson, & Day, 2015). The impact of out-of-home placement on a family is substantial; it is traumatic and has a negative influence on, for example, academic performances of youths. The positive effect of out-of-home placement on children's psychological functioning is modest at best (De Swart et al., 2012). Therefore, and as also stated in the international Convention on the Rights of the Child (United Nations [UN], 1990), out-of-home-placement should be a last resort option (Dozier et al., 2014; Whittaker, Del Valle, & Holmes, 2015).

As the expansion of the social network through the involvement of professionals is temporary and the influence is limited, especially during out-of-home placement, alternatives to out-of-home placement are needed. Collaborating with the social network of the family may offer more sustainable solutions. In particular, we assume that collaborating with an informal mentor can offer a new way to make use of existing connections and expand their transferal, resulting in more continuity and better client participation during treatment. The case described below offers a powerful illustration of the influence of natural mentors.

> The influence of a natural mentor
> Suraya is 17 years old and has Autism and a psychotic vulnerability. A request for independent living training is pending, because Suraya wishes to live on her own. She is on a waiting list and will be granted a place in a few months. Meanwhile, life at home is characterised by flaming rows. Finally, the family supervisor advises the parents to call the police and turn her out of the house if things get of hand again. The parents agree.
> Aside from the family supervisor, other people in the environment are involved with the family. At the start of the counselling process, Suraya indicated that her best friend's mother always supported her. This mother (Kim) is asked if she is prepared to support Suraya as her YIM, which she gladly accepts. When Kim then finds out what the family supervisor has advised Suraya's parents to do, she calls the care workers in anger. She considers it unacceptable for a family supervisor to give such advice, and she wants to talk with her parents. The care worker asks her what she wants to say to them. "I want to remind them of their responsibility as parents. There is only a little while to go before Suraya can move out – how can you turn out your own child in those circumstances?" Kim asks the care workers to be present at the discussion. She is prepared to do it on her own, but she thinks that she would be able to explain things to

the parents better if the care workers are there to support her. The care worker discusses this with her team, and after weighing the various possible scenarios they decide to support Kim and pre-empt any potential escalation.

When Kim tells the parents in clear terms that she believes they simply cannot turn their daughter out now, they respond that they feel understood. They do not want to kick Suraya out at all, but they're at their wits' end. "So when professionals then advise you to turn your child out, then you just go along with that." The discussion is continued with the creation of a safety plan that incorporates multiple de-escalation measures to prevent the situation at home from reaching a breaking point again. When asked why Kim's words led the parents to change tack so drastically, they respond: "She's also taking care of our child, so isn't it natural to listen to her?"

Theoretical background of the YIM approach

Adolescence, complex needs, and the need for supportive relationships

Supportive social relationships, particularly perceived social support and social integration, are generally recognised as beneficial for individuals' health (Cohen, 2004). Social support concerns a social network's provision of psychological and material resources intended to benefit an individual's ability to cope with stress (House & Kahn, 1985). Social support eliminates or reduces the effects of stressful experiences by promoting effective coping strategies, such as less threatening interpretations of adverse events (Kawachi & Berkman, 2001). Social integration reflects participation in a broad range of social relationships and promotes positive psychological states, such as self-worth and positive affect, which induce health-promoting physiological responses (Brisesette, Cohen, & Seeman, 2000). Social integration is thought to provide information and to be a source of motivation and social stimulation to care for oneself (Cohen, 2004). Negative social interactions, on the other hand, may elicit psychological stress and physiological concomitants that increase risks for disease (Cacioppo et al., 2002).

During adolescence youths re-examine the way in which they express experiences and feelings to their parents (Keijsers et al., 2010) in order to develop their autonomy and independence and a more equal relationship with their parents (Branje et al., 2013). This developmental task is related to another task, namely, to create and maintain supportive relationships with other adolescents (De Goede, Branje, & Meeus, 2009) and non-parental adults. Non-parental adults can be supportive individuals with informal or formal status who are a natural part of the family's social environment (Kesselring et al., 2016). Longitudinal research (Werner, 1993, 2005) has shown that youths who formed bonds with supportive non-parental adults are more resilient: the bond buffers against risk factors, which is confirmed by a meta-analysis (Zolkoski & Bullock, 2012). Research indicates that vulnerable juveniles find it difficult to establish positive natural relationships due to low self-esteem, lack of trust and social skills deficits (Ahrens et al., 2011).

Effective collaboration with social networks

Integrating professional involvement with informal mentoring is thought to stimulate shared decision-making between families, their social network and professionals, and it enhances client participation. This idea of shared decision-making and participation is in line with the concept of the educative civil society, in which the joint activities of citizens in the upbringing of children and adolescents are emphasised (De Winter, 2008). The effectiveness of activities aimed to realise an educative civil society with a focus on meeting, dialogue, enhancing neighbourhood climate and network formation, are promising (Kesselring, Winter, Horjus, & Yperen, 2013). Shared decision-making with the social network means that the learning goals are created with and embedded in the family's social network, which is thought to result in personal goals that are selected for autonomous reasons (Koestner, Lekes, Powers, & Chicoine, 2002). These self-concordant goals increase goal-directed efforts, and thereby facilitate development in juveniles (Vasalampi, Salmela-Aro, & Nurmi, 2009). However, shared decision-making with the social network may not always yield positive effects. For instance, a recent meta-analysis did not find robust empirical evidence for the effectiveness of family group conferences – a process led by family members to plan and make decisions for a child who is at risk for maltreatment – and even reported non-anticipated results that may even be evaluated as negative from a family preservation perspective, such as an increase in the number and length of out-of-home placements with older children and minority groups (Dijkstra, Creemers, Asscher, Dekovic, & Stams, 2016). Such lack of positive effects may be explained by the collaboration of too many persons (i.e. all relevant social network members), because research shows that teams with more than five individuals perform worse than smaller teams (Mueller, 2012).

A more effective way of collaborating with multi-problem families and their social network might be to start with asking the juvenile in need to nominate a Youth Initiated Mentor. Working with a YIM requires a functional position of the YIM. From a social psychology perspective, this reduces the possibility of social loafing: the presence of others results in less effort (Liden, Wayne, Jaworski, & Bennett, 2004). Although, if the positioning of this person is not accepted by the family, social network and professionals, his or her input can backfire on the results of the team (Harré et al., 2009). This process of positioning is a so-called top-down process, which includes setting a group structure, and developing norms and routines that regulate collective behaviour in ways that enhance the quality of coordination and collaboration (Woolley, Aggarwal, & Malone, 2015). Top-down processes facilitate collective intelligence, or the general ability of a group to perform well across a wide range of different tasks (Woolley, Chabris, Pentland, Hashmi, & Malone, 2010). The YIM approach translates those insights into a methodology, to create lasting and functional pedagogical alliances between the family and its social network.

The YIM approach embedded in a treatment context

Relationships with non-parental adults might serve as informal and natural mentoring relationships, and are a predictor of adolescent health (DuBois & Silverthorn, 2005). Taking advantage of and strengthening these existing supportive relationships in working with vulnerable youth recently received attention in America as an intervention strategy, designated as YIM (Schwartz et al., 2013; Spencer et al., 2016). In our case, the YIM approach is embedded in a systemic treatment approach in which access, mobilisation and consultation of informal mentors are central aspects, also known as the InConnection team.

The InConnection team works with a specialised care approach, and aims to increase resilience and prevent (repetition of) out-of-home placements in at-risk youth. The InConnection team has two features that distinguish it from care as usual. First, it involves care provided by a multidisciplinary team, consisting of professionals specialised in youth and family care, psychiatry, addiction care, and care for people with mild intellectual disabilities. The InConnection team thereby extends other integral care approaches, as it does not only include a case manager who coordinates care from different organisations or types of expertise, but it brings the different types of expertise and care together within one approach and team. This approach thus offers families' direct access to a wide range of specialised treatment possibilities, depending on the family's needs. Examples are youth-focused treatments, such as cognitive behavioural therapy and psychomotor therapy; caregiver and family-focused treatments, such as parent training, trauma therapy and multisystem treatments, including multisystemic therapy. Despite the different forms of treatment, families experience continuity of care since treatments are coherently organised to meet the family's needs and preferences. By integrating (mental) health care treatment effects and efficiency, quality of life, and client satisfaction may be improved (Valentijn, Schepman, Opheij, & Bruijnzeels, 2013).

Second, during the first phase of the InConnection team, youth nominate a YIM from the supportive adults within their social networks. The YIM is a confidant and spokesperson for the youth, and a partner for parents and professionals. During treatment, all members of the client system, including the YIM, actively participate in the decision-making process by giving their perspectives on desired treatment goals and contributing to the achievement of these goals. Thus, the collaboration with the YIM may increase shared decision-making with the family members, and through this enhance treatment effects.

> Smoking weed and a beer here and there, you know how it goes, and then he gets angry if you say something about it. I'm still allowed to say something about it though, because I'm his aunt and that makes me cool, in his eyes.
>
> (YIM, 43)

Four phases of the YIM approach

The YIM approach is characterised by four phases. The total duration of the treatment is between 6 and 9 months. The overall duration and the duration of each separate phase depends on the complexity of the problems, the motivation and possibilities of the family members, the social network and the professionals to collaborate with each other. We first describe the four phases in general, after which we describe some aspects in more detail.

Phase 1 is focused on "who": which member of the social network can become the YIM? The professionals seek collaboration with an informal mentor by stimulating youth to nominate a person in their environment they trust (*eliciting*). After nomination, the YIM is *informed* about the YIM-position and *agreements* are made about privacy, termination and the type of support he or she provides when *installed* as "the YIM". Phase 2 is focused on "what": what is everyone's perspective on the current and desired situation? By means of shared decision-making, youth, parents, YIM, and professionals *analyse* the individual and family problems and describe productive solutions that respect the family members' autonomy. Phase 3 is focused on "how": each participant can contribute to the desired situation. All participants provide advice about how to collaborate, and a plan is made in which the *learning goals* and *efforts* to reach those goals are described and acted upon. The plan serves as a *monitoring* tool during the enactment of the plan. Phase 4 is focused on "adaptivity", that is, the degree to which the current informal pedagogical alliance can meet new challenges? When all involved parties agree the *social environment* or family members' *self-regulation* secures safety of the adolescent, and promotes his or her development (Saxe, Ellis, & Brown, 2015), which could make professional care unnecessary.

During the final meeting the parties discuss the system's adaptivity – how will the family and YIM deal with new challenges, and can the informal pedagogical alliance do its work if necessary – and they make agreements about the professional's availability. Usually, the family is allowed to reach out to the professionals during the next months if necessary. A good working alliance and a continuous process of shared decision-making between

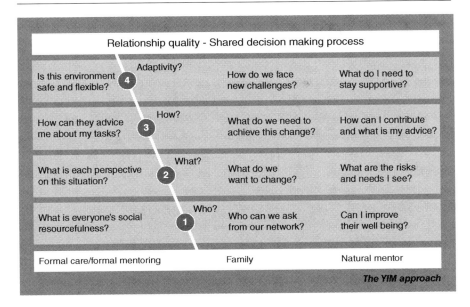

Figure 5.1 The four phases of the YIM approach.

all involved parties are crucial in all four phases. The phases, described from the perspectives of the formal involvement (professionals), family and natural mentor, are illustrated in Figure 5.1, in which the direction is emphasised to the extent that formal involvement decreases with increasing informal problem ownership.

The YIM approach focuses on reducing psychological and behavioural problems of youth and his or her family, and is meant to increase resilience. The overall goal is to create adaptive informal pedagogical alliances with enough collective intelligence to cope with new stressful situations and work on productive solutions that respect the family members' autonomy.

The YIM-approach has implications for the total process of professional care, including diagnostics and treatment. Creating sustainable decision-making partnerships between family and the social network becomes an integral and continuous part of treatment (Walker Bishop, Pullmann, & Bauer, 2015). The professional uses knowledge and techniques from position theory to realise a positioning of the youth initiated mentor that is viable for all participants (Harré et al., 2009), and from systemic theory to create lasting and healthy informal partnerships (Bronfenbrenner & Morris, 2007). The professional stimulates the family members' social resourcefulness, that is, family members' covert and overt behaviour to request and maintain support from others (Rapp et al., 2010). Enhancing social resourcefulness is meant to optimise capacity of the involved adolescents to cope with stressful life events.

Professionals need to be flexible and responsive to each unique relationship, because of differences in quality, intensity and nature of the relationship between the informal mentor and juvenile. The kind of support the YIM offers depends on the capacities, needs and interests of both the mentor and the mentee (juvenile), the individual and family problems and type of support the mentee needs, and the fit between the two persons. In general, the type of support consists of five basic elements: social emotional support (e.g. providing a listening ear), practical support (e.g. support with writing an application letter), guidance and advice (e.g. regarding work or education), role modelling (including normative guidance), and social capital (providing access to a supportive social network) (Spencer et al., 2016).

The first phase described more in detail

The first phase of the YIM approach focuses on "the Who" and raises the most questions, because normal treatment approaches mostly focus on "the What": what is the problem? At home? At school? In the neighbourhood? In this part, we describe this shift from what to whom more in depth, with practical suggestions.

The YIM (Youth Initiated Mentor) is a person who is already part of the family's natural network, who already knows the family and the situation and has shown involvement before. The YIM is asked to advise and support the juvenile, serve as a confidant and, if possible, offer shelter in crisis situations. The YIM is also invited to advise the professionals on the appropriate kind of treatment and approach and, where possible, to offer insights into the issues at play. The YIM and the family are supported by a team of professionals from various disciplines and organisations, with experts from the fields of psychiatry, addiction services, care for the mildly mentally impaired and youth services. These professionals work according to a shared vision, and they visit the juvenile and the family in their own setting, unless it is more appropriate to carry out a treatment at a different location. In addition to their role as treatment providers, the professionals can also act as directors (holder of ultimate responsibility and mediator between the family and the network). The professionals do not view problems as isolated units, but as a network of interrelated factors that have a function within the family or the broader social network.

Professional involvement according to the YIM approach means that the professional cannot act on his own. An integrative part of the treatment is cooperation with the available informal expertise. The treatment offered by the professional (such as family discussions, cognitive behavioural therapy or other therapeutic talks) is enriched by the knowledge that social network members have of the issues. At the same time, the professional works on improving the functioning of the social network where necessary; the social network is seen as the context in which the treatment takes place, and this context is of crucial importance to treatment. This means that cooperation with the social network is an integrative part of professional involvement.

During the first phase, the professional makes it clear that he is not nearly as effective on his own as when he can cooperate with a YIM. This leads to a discussion with the family members about the added value of a YIM, what introducing a YIM means for them as a family and for everyone individually, including the YIM and the professional. This is a crucial phase, because it involves a different start than other treatment programmes: consideration is first given to the question of who can help, to address the actual problem only in phase two. A juvenile recounts what this meant for him:

> The YIM was already involved. That collaboration made her role clearer, which made it possible for discussions to go just that much deeper. Let me be a bit more open. I know I can rely on her and what I can talk to her about.
>
> (Robin, 16)

This first phase can also be difficult, however, as the following testimony by a juvenile's parents shows:

FATHER: There had to be a YIM, even if we had to pull one out of thin air.
MOTHER: We were even told that if I could not find a YIM, we'd get a different form of help. That went down badly with me. We were already so involved by that time, it would be terrible if that were to happen.
FATHER: They should make two models, one in case there is a YIM and one if there isn't. We can ask as many people as we want, but if there's no one among them that appeals to our son, well, we can't conjure up a YIM.

The professionals, family and informal mentor are a single team whose objective is to bring an end to the problems in question or to make them manageable. Each team member has a different role and different tasks, and each team member's contribution is relevant. Without a YIM, the team is incomplete; hence, the first goal is "find a YIM". The YIM is crucial for several reasons. The presence of a "familiar outsider" serves, for example, to interrupt existing patterns of interaction between the family members. Furthermore, it increases motivation: because the juvenile is allowed to choose his YIM, he feels like he has more say in matters. The other family members, meanwhile, feel that they and the people around them are being listened to. By coordinating the treatment with an informal mentor, multiple persons commit to the chosen solution path, creating a greater support base. Also, the informal mentor brings a new dimension to the treatment programme: he can inform the team of the parents' child-raising ideals, adding a normative input that the professionals lack.

Experience shows that allegiance is another essential requirement for the success of this approach. By allegiance, we mean the professional's conviction that this approach will help the family at this time (Barnhoorn et al., 2013). In our experience, if the professional is not personally convinced of the added value of a YIM, the family registers this and tends to choose the familiar route, that is, to solve problems with the help of professionals. This allegiance is also necessary in order to be able to set standards in the team's work: "We really need a YIM for this treatment team to be complete". If you are unconvinced of the value of a YIM, you are asking a family to do something that you yourself do not believe in, and that is not effective. The combination of being convinced of your approach and setting a clear standard ensures that families are often able to appoint a YIM, even when they or previously involved professionals originally did not believe they would succeed. This combination also sends the message that professionals are not the solution, but that they can help family members help themselves and each other.

Situations exist in which there is such a degree of insecurity that an intervention with professional expertise must be carried immediately to safeguard the juvenile's safety. Usually, these situations are highly conducive to finding a YIM, because people in the environment are often concerned about the juvenile. Too much professional expertise in this phase can give families the feeling that they will get the help they need anyway, with or without a YIM. It is therefore important to be aware of this, and to "thematise" any problems with finding a YIM. By this, we mean to openly address these problems. If there is a sense of shame or embarrassment involved, then this should be addressed. If the family says they have no network, it should be emphasised how painful and difficult that is. If the youth is nervous about appointing someone because he is afraid to hurt his parents, this should also be discussed. In short, every individual obstacle is open to discussion in order to remove it. This is a very delicate process, in which the security of the family members and their environment is a minimum (necessary) condition that must be maintained at all times.

Step 1: addressing network motivation

One of the first questions asked during a juvenile's intake is: "Is it okay if someone in your environment becomes part of this programme?" The principle of the YIM is explained to the juvenile as "someone you trust, who you can turn to for support and advice, and/or someone who inspires you to try your hardest."

Based on our experience and interviews with families and YIMs, we have found that a YIM is most effective when he:

- is a trusted confidant to the juvenile and the parents feel supported by him;
- is not paid for his efforts;

- can identify various perspectives in a situation and can address these openly;
- is capable of making clear agreements and keeping them;
- has an objective, determined together with the juvenile and parents;
- is capable of dealing conscientiously with the information he becomes privy to;
- can deal with the difference in roles as informal supportive figure and as "uncle, grandma, or neighbour"; and
- is able to "be there", both physically and emotionally, with a frequency determined by himself and the juvenile.

In practice, not all these factors for success can always be met, and it is up to the parents and professionals to deviate from them, purposefully and based on their expertise.

It is important for families to get into a "yes" mood during this first step; that they say "yes" to sharing their problems with the environment and that they recognise that the support will not be as effective without the involvement of people in their environment. We see the involvement of a YIM as a precondition for success; this view is explained by providing psychoeducation about "cooperation with the social network". This can be summarised in five main points, listed here with a number of examples of how professionals can explain them to family members.

The YIM approach is:

1. Lasting: an informal mentor can contribute ideas based on his life experience and experience with the family, and will, in principle, be involved longer than a professional.

    Example explanations:
    - "People around you know you best, they know what would work for you and what wouldn't."
    - "Care workers are around only for a short while, they'll leave once you no longer need care. A YIM has often been around for a while already and will continue to be there afterwards, so he or she can give support for longer."
    - "People in the background are often already aware of what's going on or can at least see that things aren't going well, and they often want to help. Involving them as a YIM lets them do something for your family."
    - "You have already received quite a lot of help, but when that help stopped, things often slowly but surely grew worse again; otherwise we wouldn't be sitting here now. With a YIM, we want to consider a long-term solution with you."

2 Familiar: the YIM is someone who knows the family and who can serve as a safe, second home for the juvenile.
   Example explanations:

   - "Because the YIM already knows you and you might already visit him often, it is good to have a place you can go to when things get out of hand at home. That way, you and your parents know that there's a safe place you can stay."
   - "Going to a YIM, or doing something fun together, can be a good distraction from your problems at home/at school etc."
   - "You've already seen so many different care workers that we can imagine that you're done with talking. Wouldn't it be great to just be able to talk things over with someone who knows you well and doesn't have to hear the whole story all over again?"

3 Influential: the informal mentor has an influence that the professionals do not have and that the parents may have lost for the time being.
   Example explanations:

   - "Many juveniles grow tired of all the talking and all the care workers. A YIM can help you figure out solutions without all the hassle."
   - "The YIM can help you come up with ideas and work on the problems. That way, you're doing it together, not alone."
   - "It's good to have someone you trust and who's really there for you."
   - "Care workers can't magically figure out what the solution is – you don't know, and neither do we. But we do believe that if we search together with you and your YIM, we can definitely find something that will really work!"

4 Appropriate to the juvenile: in this phase of life, juveniles redefine how they share experiences and feelings with their parents (Keijsers et al., 2010), and it is proper for them to build a relationship with an adult other than their parents (Beyers & Goossens, 1999; Steinberg, 1990).
   Example explanations:

   - "Many juveniles don't (want to) share everything with their parents anymore. That's a normal part of growing up."
   - "Maybe you want your parents to mind their own business. It's still nice to have another adult who knows you well to be there for you and figure things out with you. Life is pretty complicated, after all."

5 Motivational: the juvenile is given more say in the programme and the YIM helps him stick to the plan.
   Example explanations:

   - "A YIM can help you put into words what is going on and how we can work on solutions."

- "The YIM can support you when things aren't going your way and encourage you to keep going."

Step 2: consideration and invitation

After raising the possibility of a YIM and explaining the added value, the parties involved should be given some time to think things over. This can literally mean that the professionals give their explanation and then leave, and the family contacts them when they have decided on a YIM. It is also possible that the family needs more help with finding a YIM, in which case that help is provided. The family can also indicate that it is not prepared to think about the question. In that case, it is up to the professional to discuss the family's network motivation nonetheless, using his expertise. He could do so by charting out the social network, for instance, and discussing who is important in what way, or simply by persevering and continuing to give support, as this juvenile's experience shows:

> It was difficult for me to ask the YIM myself. She has two jobs, and on top of that she'd have to go to a discussion with me and a bunch of care workers. I found it difficult to burden her with that. But in the end, I did ask. It was no simple matter, but the care workers kept asking me about it and eventually I just gathered up my courage and did it. After that, the care workers explained the whole YIM story to her, because I couldn't explain it properly myself.
>
> (Ilse, 15)

This consideration process is a process for the juvenile and the family. They both have to support the choice of a potential YIM, as a juvenile describes:

> I believe we should all decide together. I couldn't choose the right person on my own, and neither could my parents.
>
> (Jayden, 14)

Indeed, parents have a very accurate idea of how they want to cooperate with a YIM:

> I don't think that the YIM should be an extension of us. It needs to be someone who can say to our son: 'You want to do something, so do something.' Someone who can set things in motion, make sure that promises aren't hollow. If our son says "I want to study," the YIM should say: "I know someone who studies such-and-such, you should talk to him." Or: "Let's go to an open day then." If we parents were to say something like that, he'd brush it aside. It has to be someone he respects.
>
> (Harry, 53)

It is advisable to further discuss the YIM choice a family ultimately makes, as professionals indicate that this often yields useful information:

> Every time, it's intriguing to see who juveniles choose to be their YIM. So far, they have always been adults who mean a lot to the juvenile. They are people who have a history with the family, and that seems to be why the juveniles choose them. Like that one uncle who didn't stay quiet and raised the issue of the sexual abuse by grandfather. Or the grandmother who, despite the divorce, still maintains a good relationship with both parents. It's almost as if the juveniles choose the YIMs because of the positive contributions that these adults have already made in their family lives.
> (Els, systemic therapist)

Step 3: explore impact and position of a potential YIM

Once the family has someone in mind for the mentor role, it is time to discuss how to approach this person. It is preferable for the juvenile himself to approach him, possibly together with the parents. Where necessary, the professional can assist. Many YIMs have the following to say about being asked:

> You feel honoured. They are putting their trust in you, and that's very special. You'd do anything for someone like that.
> (Sophie, 47)

Naturally, we want to take advantage of this power, but we also want to prevent that the YIM says "yes" only out of emotion or due to social pressure. We want to support the potential YIM in rationally thinking it over, because we believe that if the choice is made both rationally and emotionally, the YIM-hood is more likely to be successful. For this reason, after the question has been asked, the professional has a discussion with the prospective YIM, together with the juvenile and/or his parents if desired and appropriate.

The objective of this discussion is to make clear what the role of the informal mentor is and to open this to discussion. For instance: that it is important that the YIM is able to gain the trust of the juvenile, the parents and the professionals, so that he can contribute to the treatment of the juvenile and the parents in his own way. He must also be able to clearly indicate his limits, so that he can keep his neutral position and avoid being overburdened. Furthermore, it must be clear to this person how the roles are divided between him and the parents, and he must be able to respect that. For that reason, it can be helpful to explain during this talk that he will no longer be just uncle or neighbour, but YIM as well. How does he feel about that? Would he dare confront the juvenile about his behaviour, advise the parents to be more strict, or blow the whistle when the professional is going too fast?

It is also explained to the YIM why his input is so important. There are several reasons why; to begin with, he knows the family, which means that professionals can learn from him about family dynamics, long-term conflicts and the manner in which all this can be broached. Furthermore, he is someone the juvenile trusts. Another important point is the influence that a YIM has on the juvenile; this influence often exists implicitly, but it is a force that should not be underestimated. The YIM also brings a new dynamic to the family. His presence can create space in the family by taking the juvenile out for a day or serving as someone to whom the juvenile can vent his feelings, and by changing the dynamic with the professionals. The family no longer has to "face" the professionals alone – someone in their environment is helping them. Individual attention for the juvenile is another important aspect. This is something that the parents often have not given him for a while, due to persistent conflicts. Finally, it is also explained that the juvenile's request is an indication of appreciation: the juvenile likes them. As such, the juvenile has put himself in a vulnerable position by making this request. If necessary, the prospective YIM is asked to handle the request with care.

All this is discussed with the prospective YIM using what we call the Levinas conversation guide, as interpreted by Dutch philosopher Jan Keij (2007, 2012). As we described in the first intermezzo, *the power of the YIM request*, the philosopher Emmanuel Levinas has written extensively about the appeal (request) from one person to another to "improve his quality of life". This appeal is often an implicit request that requires a choice, which creates a dilemma. Think, for example, of when you see a homeless person selling newspapers, or when the lift doors start to close and someone comes running in to reach it before it closes. These are moments where, often, nothing is said, yet you may still feel uncomfortable. Will you buy a newspaper? Do you block the door with your foot so that the other person can get in? In the informal mentor's situation, this appeal has often been present for a while; for instance, at a family party, an uncle chatted with his nephew, about whom he has heard stories of dropping out of school and drug abuse. "Should I or shouldn't I talk to him about his education?" By asking the juvenile to explicitly formulate a request for help towards a person he trusts, this dilemma is opened to discussion.

The Levinas conversation guide comprises the following questions aimed at discussing the prospective YIM's dilemma:

- What does this request for help mean for your own role and needs?
- How do you interpret this request?
- What activities, contacts or convictions would you have to let go of, if you accepted this request?
- Are there conditions that must be met for you to be able to do this? Do you expect something from the juvenile, the family, professionals or supportive figures around you?

In practice, these questions are not discussed as though checking off a list; rather, it is a natural process. The questions serve as a reference and reminder for the professional, not as a questionnaire. After the discussion, the prospective YIM considers the request and makes his decision known. Several discussions may be necessary before a YIM definitively accepts its role.

The positioning theory (Harré, 2009) can be of help in this third step of phase 1, in discussing to what extent the YIM's position is effective. This theory aims to clarify explicit and implicit patterns of reasoning that express themselves in interactions between people. It explores the positions of all involved parties, which were created as the parties assigned positions to others or themselves through previous implicit and explicit actions. These actions mark the position that someone "owns", which is local, temporary and short-lived. In other words: a person's position can be different in every new situation and can be addressed at any time. The YIM approach explicates this positioning process, the objective being for all parties present to recognise each other's positions.

A position is the attitude a person takes in a social system (Procter, 1985, in Neimeyer & Mahoney, 1995). As a person goes through experiences, he bases his position on his reflections on: (1) his view of himself, (2) how others think, and (3) his reflections on (1) and (2). During this step, the professional explains his intervention by clarifying the positioning process that takes place within all family members and their social network. By choosing a YIM, the juvenile changes the existing positions.

The positioning theory assumes the following:

- Rights and obligations are exchanged between people in variable patterns when they undertake activities together;
- The resulting patterns form the process of positioning, through which rights and obligations are assigned or refused;
- The activities are meaningful and can be interpreted in several ways;
- The power of each activity, if it is recognised by the persons involved, determines a person's position, and thus influences the position of the other persons involved.

Choosing a YIM is an activity that makes the existing morality open to discussion: what are the beliefs and approaches of all the parties in this complex situation? What rights and obligations are attributed to whom?

Positioning theory identifies three positions that can be taken. The first-order position is the *candidate status* for a position. This can be an uncle who the juvenile has in mind for the role of YIM, simply because he has an extended history of positive contact with him. The candidate status does not offer much in the way of influence; it is more of a side-line position. The second-order position is an implicitly or explicitly *accepted position*. This could be the mother of a friend with whom both daughter and parents have a good relationship. The mothers share experiences and the daughter occasionally finds a listening ear in her friend's mother. Both the daughter and her mother agree that she is a supportive figure to them. However, she had never been positioned as such – things simply grew this way. The third position is someone with *footing*. This is someone who can give his opinion, even unasked, and is listened to. This is the most desirable situation for a YIM, as this position means that he is recognised by all those involved and has influence. It is important to have a YIM in a third-order position, because this is someone who can contribute to the collaboration process. With a first or second-order YIM, the positions of the different parties must first be recognised for collaboration to become possible.

YIMs have indicated the following about a YIM with footing, that is, a "good YIM." They say that a good YIM must be able to understand both sides, that is, the parents and the juvenile. He must be able to empathise with both sides of the story. Furthermore, he must be able to foster understanding between the parents and the child. He can do this by helping them understand the situation and talking about how individuals act and why. A YIM must be someone who can make clear agreements and stick to them, as this creates trust. It must be someone who, with the juvenile, has a goal in mind and is prepared to work towards it with him. He must be able to maintain anonymity towards third parties: "this stays between us". If relevant, he must be able to deal with the different positions: "grandfather and YIM", "neighbour and YIM", etc. At last but not least, it has to be someone who has a bond with the juvenile and can get along with the parents.

When YIMs are asked what they need in order to fulfil their role well; they have the following to say. They want to see progress, or that their input is effective. They want to have the parent's faith in their ability and, preferably, to be able to work together with the parents as well. They want professionals to reinforce their position, for instance by indicating that the YIM's input is crucial to the success of the collaboration. They want to be able to distance themselves from the situation from time to time, and they want to be able to consult professionals and vent their frustrations, and to have the option to call the professional they are acquainted with.

The following case illustrates a situation in which there is a second-order YIM, and efforts are made to achieve a third-order YIM.

Who can help?

> The parents want Sander (17, diagnosed with ODD, ADHD and Autism) out of the house. He is aggressive and terrorises the other family members, which is not good for the three younger children. During the introduction, Sander is asked who, other than his parents, is important to him, who he could turn to for support and advice. He immediately names Cor. His parents nod; Cor is his former work experience supervisor and has since become something of a friend to Sander. Would Sander be prepared to ask Cor to support him in his desire to stay at home? Sander smiles broadly and says he doesn't mind asking.

On a visit to Cor, Sander explains – in the presence of professionals – that things are not going well at home, but he does not want to leave the house.

Would Cor be prepared to help him with that? Cor nods, but before anything else he wants to make clear that Sander's parents are not in their right minds. They don't know their own son, and they don't take him seriously. He has never heard the boy speak a cross word! And they claim that he's a terror at home? In Cor's view, it's the other way round. Sander's parents aren't seeing him with their hearts. They use him to express their anger, and as a result they see nothing but bad things in him. The professionals talk with Cor and Sander about how Sander feels about hearing Cor describe his parents so negatively. Sander knows Cor's opinion, and he finds it difficult. It makes him feel stuck in the middle – he likes both Cor and his parents, and feels supported by both as long as they're not at odds with each other. Does Cor intend to continue to express himself negatively about Sander's parents in the future? "No, I just wanted to get this off my chest, and with that done, I'm there for Sander. No more, no less."

When feedback is given to the parents, it turns out they expected this reaction from Cor. The reason why they nevertheless agreed to the proposal to appoint Cor as YIM is that they want the best for their son, and they can see that Cor has an influence that they no longer have. As such, they are open to having him help determine the treatment objectives and to support Sander where necessary. An action plan has since been created for Sander to which both his parents and Cor have agreed. Part of this plan is that the contact between the parents, Cor and Sander will be examined regularly.

Step 4: mounting the soapbox

An informal mentor is someone from the social network who temporarily mounts a soapbox: he does not move from where he is standing, but his influence does increase. It is important to mark that moment, that it is recognised and acknowledged that this person is allowed to temporarily take up the position of a YIM. For that, it is important to discuss the following subjects:

- *Confidentiality*: What does the YIM tell the parents and professionals about his interaction with the juvenile?
- *Privacy*: What are professionals allowed to discuss with the YIM about the family?
- *Contact frequency*: How often does contact occur between the juvenile and the YIM, the parents and the YIM and the professionals and the YIM?
- *Boundaries*: What does the YIM not want to be involved in, and what does the family not want to involve the YIM in?
- *Worst case scenario*: What if things do not go well and the parties want to end the collaboration? How will the professionals then wrap things up properly?

The marking of this moment is effected through a ritual that affirms the role of the YIM as the ambassador of the juvenile. Professionals can shape this ritual as they see best: what suits them and the family? Some professionals do it by asking the juvenile why he wants this person to be his YIM, after which the parents are asked for explicit approval of this person as YIM, and finally the question is put to the YIM: "Do you want to work with us to help … in the following months?" Once everyone has answered, the professional says something along the lines of: "Then you are now officially the YIM of …". In other cases, the signing of the plan of approach (the next step) by all the parties serves as the moment of definitive confirmation of the collaboration.

Practical matters

Discussions should preferably be held at home, or if the juvenile no longer lives there, at his temporary accommodation. This is because home visits yield much useful information about the juvenile's living environment, family composition and other relevant issues. The intake should preferably be conducted by a pair of professionals and must be discussed in advance with the methodology coach (the systemic therapist in the team who ensures the proper implementation of methodology) or by the team. The results are also discussed with the methodology coach or with the team.

After approximately 3 weeks, the professionals and the family discuss whether the treatment is a good fit and a go or no go decision is made. If the joint conclusion is that the form of care is not suited for the family, the professionals and the family consider other care options that might be more suitable, and they are transferred in a personal and caring manner. This means that the family is supervised and assisted until the new care has started.

Rules of thumb for working effectively with the YIM approach

The YIM approach is a generic working method that can be integrated into other processes, such as collaborating with juveniles in specialist care, community care or schools. It is not a separate module, such as cognitive behavioural therapy (CBT), system therapy or Eye Movement Desensitization and Reprocessing (EMDR). The difference between the YIM approach and modules such as these is that they form *one part* of a (treatment) plan. Working with informal mentors is an integrated part of the *entire* plan. It is therefore important when working with informal mentors to do so from the very outset, as doing otherwise will not allow for a sufficient level of equality among the collaborators during the plan. Introducing an informal mentor halfway through or towards the end of a plan could create the impression that this person is being introduced "because the professional will be leaving eventually"; however, the YIM approach is also intended to expand a relationship that *is* long-term. At the same time, given the complexity of the issues, it is intended as an acknowledgement that interventions such as CBT, system therapy and EMDR are less efficient in the absence of an informal mentor.

How, then, does one give shape to this cooperation in an effective way? What are the minimal requirements that must be met for the YIM approach to be effective? We have formulated a number of rules of thumb that professionals can use to monitor how well they are keeping to the method (see Table 5.1). We advise each professional to complete the form shown below twice per year, once together with a family and informal mentor with whom he feels that the cooperation is going well, and once with a family and informal mentor with whom he feels that the cooperation could be better. The subsequent discussion of the form with colleagues serves as a reflection on the actions of the professionals. Afterwards, he and his colleagues together reflect on this discussion with the family and informal mentor.

The implementation of the YIM approach in existing forms of care can be a challenge. Especially in youth care aimed at multi-problematic youth, the overall treatment goal tends to be the reparation or amelioration of a juveniles disruptive behaviour. The juvenile needs to change or needs protection. Treatment is usually a way to achieve both. Youth care professionals in existing forms of care, and therefore working in existing care systems, can encounter many difficulties in working with YIM, even when adhering to the rules of thumb.

Although the aim of YIM is to prevent an out of home placement, the stress reducing and empowering effect of a YIM may also be useful to shorten an out of home placement. In secure youth care in the Netherlands, juveniles are placed out of home following a (systemic) safety crisis, in which the juvenile is deemed to be severe at risk (i.e. is the victim of abuse) or his or her surrounding is at risk because of the juveniles behaviour (i.e. the juvenile displays severe harmful, transgressive behaviour). This crisis may not, to the perception of the responsible adults involved, be stopped in any other way than an out of home placement, safety first. As mentioned before, a crisis however, is usually an opportune moment for finding a YIM. Being empowered to choose a confidant, who can help you through the experience and relieve stress, could be thought of as a very important first step to recovery. This however proves to be a difficult point of view. Many of the involved responsible adults (parents and professionals) may have lost or have low trust in decisions of the juvenile. "The aim of placement and treatment being to influence the juvenile, to take the lead, and to keep him/her safe." Directly minimising the influence of the care professional by stating that there is someone else out there that is needed to be effective, might not feel so empowering to the care professional. The first question that often comes up is "How can a very problematic juvenile choose someone that can help them?", a sign of low allegiance. Most professionals feel that they are the ones that need to help the juvenile. This conviction may also not just be a private mindset, but a foundation of the youth care system. When implementing YIM in existing forms of care, it is therefore crucial to assess to what aim this care form exists/is used in the broader context. What underlying assumptions are made about what has to be achieved? If the overall goal of an intervention

Table 5.1 Rules of thumb for professionals to use the YIM approach effectively

	Criterion	Yes	No	Reflection
Phase 1 Intake	1. I managed to start this cooperation with the question as to which person in the family's social network can assist (phase 1)			
	2. The family has noticed that I perceive an added value in working with informal mentors (phase 1, steps 1.1, & 1.2)			
	3. I have discussed with the family and informal mentor what will change for them if they decide to work together in this manner (phase 1, step 1.3)			
	4. We have described the cooperation agreements between the family, informal mentor and myself, the professional (phase 1, step 1.4)			
	5. The juvenile chose an informal mentor within 30 days			
Phase 2 Analysis	6. I have discussed everyone's possibilities plus the inter-dynamics and the function of the cooperation with the family and the informal mentor (phase 2, step 1)			
	7. I have drawn up an analysis of the problems and the solution approach with the family and the informal mentor (phase 2, step 2)			
Phase 3 Implementation	8. I have formulated learning objectives with the family and the informal mentor (phase 3, step 1)			
	9. I have discussed the division of tasks with the family and the informal mentor (phase 3, step 2)			
	10. The collaboration plan that we drew up describes: • The agreements between the informal mentor, juvenile, parents and professionals about confidentiality, privacy, frequency of contact, limits and how to act if the cooperation between the informal mentor and the family hits a bump • The actions of family members, social network and professionals • The intended changes to be achieved and the time within which they are to be achieved.			

(Continued)

Table 5.1 Rules of thumb for professionals to use the YIM approach effectively (Continued)

	Criterion	Yes	No	Reflection
Phase 4 Conclusion	11. I have evaluated the learning objectives with the family and the informal mentor (phase 4, step 1)			
	12. I have made agreements with the family and the informal mentor about how they can hold on to what we have achieved (phase 4, step 2)			
	13. I have made agreements with the family and the informal mentor about the form that the informal mentor's involvement will take from now on and how they can ask for my assistance if their cooperation stagnates (phase 4, step 2)			
Overall Cooperative relationship	14. If the family did not perceive any added value in cooperating with the social network or professional network, I demonstrated understanding for that			
	15. If the family did not think that anything needed to change or did not have positive feelings about it, I demonstrated understanding for that			
When out-of-home placement could no longer be prevented, we went through the following steps:	16. I have discussed the situation with all people involved			
	17. Based on that discussion and the preceding collaboration, I have mapped out the risk factors and protection factors			
	18. Using the trauma system model, I have made a safety estimation			
	19. I have written down the above			
	20. I have discussed my considerations and my proposal with the treatment team (the formal and informal experts)			
	21. I have described the purpose and expected duration of the out-of-home placement			
Learning cycle	22. With the team, we organise meetings with the families and the informal mentors twice a year, to talk about ways to improve our cooperation			

is to increase resilience in the social network and to empower the juvenile, than working with YIM is a logical addition. If this is not (yet) the case, a discussion about a paradigm shift with care system partners needs to take place first, to support individual professionals in working with YIM and applying the rules of thumb.

Effectiveness of the YIM approach

In the Netherlands, we investigated whether YIM is a feasible ambulatory alternative for adolescents for whom out-of-home placement is indicated (Van Dam et al., 2017). This study focused on the questions if youth can nominate a natural mentor, if out-of-home placement could be prevented and if the problems of adolescents with a YIM were comparable to the problems experienced by a residential population of youth with complex needs. A total of 83% of the juveniles in the YIM group ($n = 96$) were able to nominate a mentor after on average 33 days. Ninety percent of the adolescents in the YIM group received ambulatory treatment as an alternative for indicated out-of-home-placement, while their problems were largely comparable with those of juveniles in Dutch semi-secure residential care. Results therefore suggest that the involvement of important non-parental adults may help to prevent out-of-home placement of adolescents with complex needs.

In a mixed methods follow-up study, we further explored the question if YIM could be a sustainable ambulatory alternative for early and late adolescents with complex needs for whom out-of-home placement is indicated (Van Dam et al., 2018). The results showed that a total of 79% of the youth ($n = 42$) succeeded in nominating a natural mentor, and 81% received solely ambulatory treatment. Youth with a natural mentor showed significantly greater declines in rule-breaking behaviour than those without a mentor, but not in leaving school or indicated out-of-home placement. Qualitative data ($n = 7$) suggested that the relationship between YIM and youth is sustainable, and that YIM might contribute to an increase of social resourcefulness and resilience. However, participants also shed light on the complex social dynamics involved when cultivating natural mentoring relationships.

In a qualitative study, we focused on the social dynamics during the YIM approach from the perspectives of the youth, parents, and YIM (Van Dam et al., 2019). This study examined how participants ($n = 19$) perceived asking someone or being asked to become YIM, what YIM needs to fulfil this position, what his or her role or tasks are, his effects on social dynamics, and the perceived sustainability of the relationship with YIM. The attitudes from participants towards asking someone or being asked to become YIM varied from enthusiastic to cautious. The majority of participants reported benefits in terms of increased contact intensity and relationship quality. One parental couple, out of six, did not experience the YIM to be beneficial. Most participants thought the YIM-mentee relationship would last after ending professional care. The results revealed that youth experience YIM as an ally during the process of receiving professional care. Nevertheless, this approach also has the potential to elicit an increase of relational conflicts between the family and social network members.

The current results provide preliminary evidence for the positive impact of a natural mentor, the transitioning process in asking, becoming, and being a YIM is valued by most participants and the YIM relationship seems to be sustainable. Nevertheless, future research should gain more insight in the different working mechanisms of the YIM approach, especially because the effectiveness of the YIM approach has not been established yet, and some negative side effects were found as well. Therefore, it should be investigated for which families and under which circumstances the YIM approach "works" and for which families and circumstances it does not work. As in general most youth interventions only work for a small subset of clients, it is necessary to also conduct research on families in which the YIM approach failed to yield positive effects. Results from such research can be used to further improve the programme theory of YIM, increase its effectiveness, and prevent negative effects of the YIM approach.

To address these gaps in the literature, a quasi-experimental study (Koper, Creemers, Branje, Stams, & van Dam, 2020) has been set up which aims to examine the effectiveness and working mechanisms of the YIM approach for youth from multi-problem families. The *Growth in personal environment* (GRIP) study will follow 300 families during youth and family care trajectories, of which 225 are treated with the YIM approach, and 75 are offered care as usual. All family members above 10 years of age, the YIM and the case manager are invited to fill in a questionnaire four times during 15 months. Additionally, 10–20 families are invited to participate in an interview study that aims to document the YIM selection process, and give insight into why most families successfully nominate a YIM, whereas others do not.

Conclusion

It seems feasible to cultivate the relationship between youth and someone they trust from within their community: a natural mentor. This relational approach ("who works principle") might improve "what works" in youth care. Future research should focus more on the different applications and the circumstances under which youth benefit the most from natural mentoring: what works for whom under which circumstances? Nevertheless, supportive relationships with the people surrounding a person generally improve health and function as a risk barrier. We therefore should provide youth with positive and hopeful relational experiences, so they are wired to recruit and become mentors themselves during lifetime.

References

Ahrens, K. R., DuBois, D. L., Richardson, L. P., Fan, M.Y., & Lozano, P. (2008). Youth in foster care with adult mentors during adolescence have improved adult outcomes. *Pediatrics*, 121, e246–e252.

Ainsworth, M. S. (1979). Infant-mother attachment. *American Psychologist*, 34, 932–937.

Anderson, H. (1990). Then and now: A journey from 'knowing' to 'not knowing'. *Contemporary Family Therapy*, 12, 193–197.

Bakker, I., Bakker, K., Dijke A. van, & Terpstra, L. (1998). *O & O in perspectief.* Utrecht, Nederlands Instituut voor Zorg en Welzijn (NIZW).

Barker, G. (2007). *Adolescent, social support and help-seeking behaviour: An international literature review and programme consultation with recommendations for action.* Geneva: WHO.

Barnhoorn, J., Broeren, S., Distelbrink, M., de Greef, M., van Grieken, A., Jansen, W ... Raat, H. (2013). *Client-, professional- en alliantiefactoren: Hun relatie met het effect van zorg voor jeugd.* Utrecht: ZonMw.

Beyers, W., & Goossens, L. (1999). Emotional autonomy, psychosocial adjustment and parenting: Interactions, moderating and mediating effects. *Journal of Adolescence, 22,* 753–769.

Bowers, E. P., Johnson, S. K., Warren, D. J. A., Tirrell, J. M., & Lerner, J. V. (2015). Youth-adult relationships and positive youth development. In E. P. Bowers, G. J. Geldhof, S. K. Johnson, L. J. Hilliard, R. M. Hershberg, J. V. Lerner, & R. M. Lerner (Eds.), *Advancing responsible adolescent development. Promoting positive youth development: Lessons from the 4-H study* (pp. 97–120). Springer International Publishing. https://doi.org/10.1007/978-3-319-17166-1_6

Brisesette, I., Cohen, S., & Seeman, T. E. (2000). Measuring social integration and social networks. In S. Cohen, L. Underwood, & B. Gottlieb (Eds.), *Measuring and intervening in social support* (pp. 53–85). New York, NY: Oxford University Press.

Bronfenbrenner, U., & Morris, P. (2007). The bioecological model of human development. In: R. M. Lerner (Ed.), *Handbook of Child Pscyhology* (pp. 795–828). New York: John Wiley and Sons.

Brugha, T. S., Weich, S., Singleton, N., Lewis, G., Bebbington, P. E., Jenkins, R., & Meltzer, H. (2005). Primary group size, social support, gender and future mental health status in a prospective study of people living in private households throughout Great Britain. *Psychological Medicine, 35,* 705–714.

Budde, S., & Schene, P. (2004). Informal social support interventions and their role in violence prevention: An agenda for future evaluation. *Journal of Interpersonal Violence, 3,* 341–355.

Burford, G. (2005). Family group conferences in the youth justice and the child welfare systems. In J. Pennell & G. Anderson (Eds.), *Widening the circle: The practice and evaluation of family group conferencing with children, young persons and their families* (pp. 203–220). Washington, DC: National Association of Social Workers Press.

Cacioppo, J. T., Hawkley, L. C., Crawford, E., Ernst, J. M., Burleson, M. H., Kowalewski, R. B., ... Berntson, Gary G. (2002) Loneliness and health: Potential mechanisms', *Psychosomatic Medicine, 64,* pp. 407–417.

Center for Promise. (2015). *Don't quit on me: What young people who left school say about the power of relationships.* Washington: America's Promise Alliance.

Choy, J. (2005). *De vraag op het antwoord: Systemische interventies voor conflicten in organisaties.* Santpoort: NISTO.

Cohen, S. (2004). Social relationships and health. *American Psychologist, 8,* 676–684.

Christakis, N. A., & Fowler, J. H. (2013). Social contagion theory: Examining dynamic social networks and human behavior. *Statistics in Medicine, 32,* 556–577. https://doi.org/10.1002/sim.5408

De Goede, I. H. A., Branje, S. J. T., & Meeus, W. H. J. (2009). Developmental changes in adolescents' perceptions of relationships with their parents. *Journal of Youth Adolescence, 38,* 75–88. https://doi.org/10.1007/s10964-008-9286-7

De Swart, J. J. W., Van den Broek, H., Stams, G. J. J. M., Asscher, J. J., Van der Laan, P. H., Holsbrink-Engels, G. A., & Van der Helm, G. H. P. (2012). The effectiveness of institutional youth care over the past three decades: A meta-analysis. *Children and Youth Services Review, 34,* 1818–1824.

Dijkstra, S., Creemers, H. E., Asscher, J. J., Dekovic, M., & Stams, G. J. J. M. (2016). The effectiveness of family group conferencing in youth care: A meta-analysis. *Child Abuse and Neglect, 62*, 100–110.

Dozier, M., Kaufman, J., Kobak, R., O'connor, T., Sagi-Schwartz, A., Scott, S., ... Zeanah, C. (2014). Consensus statement on group care for children and adolescents: A statement of policy of the American Orthopsychiatric Association. *American Journal of Orthopsychiatry, 84*(3), 219–225. https://doi.org/10.1037/ort0000005

DuBois, D. L., & Silverthorn, N. (2005). Natural mentoring relationship and adolescent health: Evidence from a national study. *American Journal of Public Health, 95*, 518–524.

Ellis, B., Fogler, J., Hansen, S., Forbes, P., Navalta, C., & Saxe, G. (2012). Trauma systems therapy: 15-month outcome and the importance of effecting environmental change. *Psychological Trauma: Theory, Research, Practice and Policy, 6*, 624–630.

Erickson, L., McDonald, S., & Elder, G. (2009). Informal mentors and education: Complementary or compensatory resources? *Sociology of Education, 82*, 344–367.

Ernst, F., Ofman, D., & Dam, L. van (2015). *Profiel netwerkgerichte groepswerker werkzaam met de JIM-aanpak*. Zeist: Youké.

Euser, S., Alink, L.R., Stoltenborgh, M., bakermans-kranenburg, M., & van IJzendoorn, M. H. (2015). A gloomy picture: A meta-analysis of randomized controlled trials reveals disappointing effectiveness of programs aiming at preventing child maltreatment. *BMC Public Health, 15*, 1068. https://doi.org/10.1186/s12889-015-2387-9

Fraser, J. S., Grove, D., Lee, M. Y., Greene, G. J., & Solovey, A. (2014). *Integrative Family and Systems Treatment (I-FAST): A strengths-based common factors approach*. New York: Oxford University Press.

Fraser, J. S., Solovey, A. D., Grove, D., Lee, M. Y., & Greene, G.J. (2012). Integrative families and systems treatment: A middle path toward integrating common and specific factors in evidence-based family therapy. *Journal of Marital and Family Therapy, 38*, 515–528.

Granovetter, M. S. (1973). The strength of weak ties. *American Journal of Sociology, 6*, 1360–1380.

Harré, R., Moghaddam, F. H., Cairnie, T. P., Rothbart, D., & Sabat, S. R. (2009). Recent advances in positioning theory. *Theory & Psychology, 19*, 5–31

Heaney, C. A., & Israel, B. A. (2002). Social support and social networks. In: K. Glanz, B. Rimer, F. Lewis (Ed.), *Health behavior and health education: Theory, research, and practice* (pp. 185–209). San Francisco: Jossey-Bass.

Henggeler, S. W., Schoenwald, S. K., Borduin, C. M., Rowland, M. D., & Cunningham, P. B. (2009). *Multisystemic therapy for antisocial behavior in children and adolescents*. New York: Guilford Press.

Hoagwood, K. E., Cavaleri, M. A., Olin, S. S., Burns, B. J., Slaton, E., Gruttadaro, D., & Hughes, R. (2009). Family support in children's mental health: A review and synthesis. *Clinical Child and Family Psychology Review*,

House, J. S., & Kahn, R. L. (1985). Measures and concepts of social support. In S. Cohen & S. L. Syme (Eds.), *Social support and health* (pp. 83–108). New York, NY: Academic Press.

Huber, M., Knottnerus, J. A., Green, L., van der Horst, H., Jadad, A. R., Kromhout, D., ... Smid, H. (2011). How should we define health? *British Medical Journal, 343*, 1–3.

Hutschemaekers, G., Tiemens, B., & Smit, A. (2006). *Weg van professionalisering: Paradoxale bewegingen in de geestelijke gezondheidszorg*. Wolfheze: GRIP.

Karen, R. (2008). Investing in children and society: What we have learned from seven decades of attachment research. In: K. K. Kline (Ed.), *Authoritative communities: The scientific case for nurturing the whole child* (pp. 103–121). New York: Springer.

Kawachi, I., & Berkman, L. F. (2001) 'Social ties and mental health', *Journal of Urban Health: Bulletin of the New York Academy of Medicine*, 78, pp. 458–467.

Keij, J. (2007). *De filosofie van Emmanuel Levinas. In haar samenhang verklaard voor iedereen.* Kampen: Uitgeverij Klement.

Keij, J. (2012). *Levinas in de praktijk. Een handleiding voor het best mogelijke helpen, privé en in de zorg.* Kampen: Uitgeverij Klement.

Keijsers, L., Branje, S. J. T., VanderValk, I. E., & Meeus, W. (2010). Reciprocal effects between parental solicitation, parental control, adolescent disclosure, and adolescent delinquency. *Journal of Research on Adolescence, 20,* 88–113.

Kendal, S., Keeley, P., & Callery, P. (2011). Young people's preferences for emotional well-being support in high school – A focus group study. *Journal of Child and Adolescent Psychiatric Nursing, 24,* 245–253.

Kesselring, M., Winter, M. de, Horjus, B., & Yperen, T. van (2013). Allemaal opvoeders in de pedagogische civil society. Naar een theoretisch raamwerk van een ander paradigma voor opgroeien en opvoeden. *Pedagogiek, 1,* 5–20.

King, E., Brown, D., Petch, V., & Wright, A. (2014). Perceptions of support-seeking in young people attending a Youth Offending Team: An interpretative phenomenological analysis. *Clinical Child Psychology and Psychiatry, 19,* 7–23.

Koestner, R., Lekes, N., Powers, T. A., & Chicoine, E. (2002). Attaining Personal Goals: Self-Concordance Plus Implementation Intentions Equals Success. *Journal of Personality and Social Psychology, 83,* 231–244.

Konijn, C., Admiraal, S., Baart, J., van Rooij, F. B., Stams, G. J. J. M., Colonnesi, C., & Assink, M. (2019). Foster care placement instability: A meta-analytic review. *Children and Youth Services Review, 96,* 483–499.

Koper, N., Creemers, H., Branje, S., Stams, G., & Dam van L. (2020). Effectiveness and working mechanisms of the InConnection Approach in Multi-Problem Families: Study protocol of a mixed-methods study. Manuscript under review.

Liden, R. C., Wayne, S., Jaworski, R., & Bennett, N. (2004). Social loafing: A field investigation. *Journal of Management, 30,* 285–304.

Luthar, S. S., Cicchetti, D., & Becker, B. (2000). The construct of resilience: A critical evaluation and guidelines for future work. *Child Development, 71,* 543–562.

McMahon, E. (2000). The externalizing conversations of Michael White: Some considerations from theory and practice. *Child Care in Practice, 4,* 349–362.

Mueller, J. S. (2012). Why individuals in larger teams perform worse. *Organizational Behavior and Human Decision Processes, 117,* 111–124.

Naert, J., Roose, R., Rapp, R. C., & Vanderplasschen, W. (2017). Continuity of care in youth services: A systematic review. *Children and Youth Services Review, 75,* 116–126.

Neimeyer, R. M., & Mahoney, M. J. (1995). Constructivism in psychotherapy, *American Psychological Association,* 15, 320–329.

Norden, T., Malm, U., & Norlander, T. (2012). Resource Group Assertive Community Treatment (RACT) as a tool of empowerment for clients with severe mental illness: A meta-analysis. *Clinical Practice and Epidemiology in Mental Health, 8,* 144–151.

Pehlivan, T., & Brummelman, J. (2015). *I'm ready: Perspectieven van jongeren op zelfredzaamheid na jeugdhulp* [I'm ready: Perspectives from youth on self-reliance after youth care]. Amsterdam: Defence for Children.

Procter, H. G. 1985. A construct approach to family therapy and systems intervention. In E. Button (Ed.), *Personal construct theory and mental health* (pp. 327–350). Beckenham, Kent: Croom Helm.

Raposa, E. B., Dietz, N., & Rhodes, J. E. (2017), Trends in volunteer mentoring in the United States: Analysis of a decade of census survey data. *American Journal of Community Psychology, 59,* 3–14. https://doi.org/10.1002/ajcp.12117

Raposa, E. B., Rhodes, J., Stams, G. J. J., Card, N., Burton, S., Schwartz, S., ... Hussain, S. (2019). The effects of youth mentoring programs: A meta-analysis of outcome studies. *Journal of youth and adolescence, 48*(3), 423–443.

Rapp, S. R., Shukamer, S., Schmidt, S., Naughton, M., & Anderson, R. (2010). Social resourcefulness: Its relationship to social support and wellbeing among caregivers of dementia victims. *Aging & Mental Health, 2,* 40–48.

Rock, S., Michelson, D., Thomson, S., & Day, C. (2015). Understanding foster placement instability for looked after children: A systematic review and narrative synthesis of quantitative and qualitative evidence. *The British Journal of Social Work, 45*(1) 177–203. https://doi.org/10.1093/bjsw/bct084

Saxe, G. N., Ellis, B. H., & Brown, A.D. (2015). *Trauma systems therapy for children and teens.* New York: Guilford Press.

Schwartz, E. O. S., Rhodes, J. E., Spencer, R., & Grossman, J. B. (2013). Youth initiated mentoring: Investigating a new approach to working with vulnerable adolescents. *American Journal of Community Psychology, 52,* 155–169.

Seikkula, J., & Arnkhil, T. E. (2006). *Dialogical meetings in social networks.* London: Karnac Publishers.

Seikkula, J., Aaltonen, J., Alakare, B., Haarakangas, K., Keränen, J., & Lehtinen, K. (2006). Five-year experience of first-episode nonaffective psychosis in open-dialogue approach: Treatment principles, follow-up outcomes, and two case studies. *Psychotherapy Research, 16,* 214–228.

Sousa, L. (2005). Building on personal networks when intervening with multiproblem poor families. *Journal of Social Work Practice, 2,* 163–179.

Sousa L., & Rodrigues, S. (2009). Linking formal and informal support in multiproblem low-income families: The role of the family manager. *Journal of Community Psychology, 5,* 649–662.

Souverein, F. A., Van der Helm, G. H. P., & Stams, G. J. J. M. (2013). Nothing works in secure residential youth care? *Children and Youth Services Review, 35,* 1941–1945.

Spencer, R., Tugenberg, T., Ocean, M., Schwartz, S. E. O., & Rhodes, J. E. (2016). "Somebody who was on my side": A qualitative examination of youth initiated mentoring. *Youth & Society, 48*(3), 402–424. https://doi.org/10.1177/0044118X13495053

Steinberg, L. (1990). Autonomy, conflict, and harmony in the family relationship. In G. R. Elliott & S. S. Feldman (Eds.), *At the threshold: The developing adolescent* (pp. 255–276). Cambridge, MA: Harvard University Press.

Stormshak, E. A., & Dishion, T. J. (2002). An ecological approach to child and family clinical and counseling psychology. *Clinical Child and Family Psychological Review, 3,* 197–215.

Strijker, J., Knorth, E. J., & Knot-Dickscheit, J. (2008). Placement history of foster care children: A study of placement history and outcomes in long-term family foster care. *Child Welfare, 87*(5), 107.

Ten Napel, J., Blanchi, F., & Bestman, M. (2006). Utilising intrinsic robustness in agricultural production systems. *Transforum Working Papers, 1,* 32–54.

Valentijn P. P., Schepman S. M., Opheij W., & Bruijnzeels M. A. (2013). Understanding integrated care: A comprehensive conceptual framework based on the integrative functions of primary care. *International Journal of Integrated Care [Internet],* 13(March):e010. Retrieved from http://www.ncbi.nlm.nih.gov/pubmed/23687482%0Ahttp://www.pubmedcentral.nih.gov/articlerender.fcgi?artid=PMC3653278

Van Dam, L., Bakhuizen, R. E., Schwartz, S. E. O., De Winter, M., Zwaanswijk, M., Wissink, I. B., & Stams, G. J. J. M. (2019). An exploration of youth–parent–mentor relationship dynamics in a youth-initiated mentoring intervention to prevent out-of-home placement. *Youth & Society, 51*(7), 915–933.

Van Dam, L., Neels, S., De Winter, M., Branje, S., Wijsbroek, S., Hutschemaekers, G., ... Stams, G. J. (2017). Youth initiated mentors: Do they offer an alternative for out-of-home placement in youth care? *The British Journal of Social Work, 47*, 1764–1780. https://doi.org/10.1093/bjsw/bcx092

Van Dam, L., Smit, D., Wildschut, B., Branje, S. J. T., Rhodes, J. E., Assink, M., & Stams, G. J. J. M. (2018). Does natural mentoring matter? A multilevel meta-analysis on the association between natural mentoring and youth outcomes. *American Journal of Community Psychology.* https://doi.org/10.1002/ajcp.12248

Vasalampi, K., Salmela-Aro, K., & Nurmi, J. E. Adolescents' self-concordance, school engagement, and burnout predict their educational trajectories. *European Psychologist, 14,* 1–10. First published online December 16, 2009. https://10.1027/1016-9040.14.4.332

Walker, S. C., Bishop, A. S., Pullmann, M. D., & Bauer, G. (2015). A research framework for understanding the practical impact of family involvement in the juvenile system: The juvenile justice family involvement model. *American Journal of Community Psychology, 56,* 408–421.

Walsh, F. (2002). A family resilience framework: Innovative practice applications. *Family Relations, 51,* 130–137.

Walsh, F. (2003). Family resilience: A framework for clinical practice. *Family Process, 42,* 1–18.

Webber, M., Huxley, P., & Harris, T. (2011). Social capital and the course of depression: Six-month prospective cohort study. *Journal of affective disorders, 129,* 149–157.

Weisz, J. R., Kuppens, S., Eckshtain, D., Ugueto, A. M., Hawley, K. M., & Jensen-Doss, A. (2013). Performance of evidence-based youth psychotherapies compared with usual clinical care: A multilevel meta-analysis. *JAMA Psychiatry, 70*(7), 750–761. https://doi.org/10.1001/jamapsychiatry.2013.1176

Whittaker, J. K., Del Valle, J. F., & Holmes, L. (2015). The current landscape of therapeutic residential care. *Therapeutic residential care for children and youth: Developing evidence-based international practice.* Philadelphia, PA: Jessica Kingsley Publishers.

Wolff, M. de, Dekker-van der Sande, F., Sterkenburg, P., & Thoomes-Vreugdenhil, A. (2014). *Richtlijn problematische gehechtheid.* Leiden: TNO Child Health.

Woolley, A. W., Aggarwal, I., & Malone, T. W. (2015). Collective intelligence and group performance. *Current Directions in Psychological Science, 24*(6), 420–424.

Woolley, A. W., Chabris, C. F., Pentland, A., Hashmi, N., & Malone, T. W. (2010). Evidence for a collective intelligence factor in the performance of human groups. *Science, 330*(6004), 686–688.

Zimmerman, M. A., Bingenheimer, J. B., & Notaro, P. C. (2002). Natural mentors and adolescent resiliency: A study with urban youth. *American Journal of Community Psychology, 30,* 221–243.

Chapter 6

Youth mentoring and multiple social support attunement

Contributions to understand youth social development and well-being

Francisco Simões, Maria Manuela Calheiros, and Madalena Alarcão

Youth mentoring is well-known to be a complex, hybrid relational context mirroring other interpersonal relationships characteristics. Mentoring blends features of parenting, such as care giving or role modelling, friendships, including mutuality or promoting a sense of belonging, or teaching, when it involves some degree of instruction. Youth mentoring intricacy goes beyond the replication of core attributes of other relational dyads. Youth mentors nurture and sustain their bonds with the mentees in a broader social ecology of co-occurring, interactive, and sometimes competing relationships (Keller, 2005; Varga & Zaff, 2017). The social ecology of relationships as a determining factor of youth mentoring quality is, however, a relatively novel topic. Dominant research efforts in youth mentoring literature have focused on understanding how categories of factors, such as mentees' and mentors' interpersonal history and social competencies to held and sustain a mentoring relationship, the influence of developmental features on youth mentoring quality, relationship traits (e.g. duration), or programmes' characteristics and implementation (relationships goals, activities, or closure) affect mentoring processes and outcomes (DuBois, Portillo, Rhodes, Silverthorn, & Valentine, 2011).

The present chapter describes a new angle to understand and measure the links between the social ecology of youth mentoring and youths outcomes, based on the concept of Multiple Social Support Attunement (MSSA). MSSA is rooted in seminal lines of research suggesting a systemic standpoint to analyse youth development in the context of supportive relationships such as youth mentoring (Keller, 2005; Keller & Blakeslee, 2013). This model focus on the consideration of complex systems properties (Alarcão, 2000; Keller, 2005) and the web of support model (Varga & Zaff, 2017). The aim of the MSSA notion is to facilitate the examination of the enactment and impact of intrapersonal patterns of multiple social support delivered by youths' most significant relationships on their development (Simões, Calheiros, & Alarcão, 2018).

The most important relationships, including mentors, are also known as anchors, which are located at different social cores; cores correspond to clusters of strong ties between certain members, forming groups such as family or friendships (Varga & Zaff, 2017).

This chapter is organised in five sections. The first one discusses the ties between the social ecology of relationships and youth positive development, scoping the contributions of the main theoretical models which have fuelled that discussion for the past decade, with a particular focus on complex systems theory (Alarcão, 2000; Keller, 2005) and the most recent advancements offered by the web of support model (Varga & Zaff, 2017). The second section brings forward the most usual measurement approaches to test the impact of multiple social support on youth development, with references to youth mentoring when the role of mentors is regarded. A third section states the gaps inherent to the study of the social ecology of youths' multiple social support and advances the notion of MSSA as an additional conceptual resource to tackle the problems that are identified. A fourth section includes a summary of findings of an ongoing Portuguese research programme which addresses the connections between of MSSA delivered by the most important relationships from diverse cores, including mentors, and youths' social development and subjective well-being. Finally, the last section lists some research, practical, and policy-making implications of a MSSA framework for the youth mentoring field.

The ecology of social relationships and youth development

Social relationships are ties fulfilling a wide array of functions such as protection, information/knowledge, or access to tangible resources, which altogether are usually labelled as social support (Sarason & Sarason, 2009). The nature, intensity, and duration of social relationships and social support are dependent of one's personal social ecology (Varga & Zaff, 2017). The bioecological model (Bronfenbrenner & Morris, 2006) promoted important breakthroughs in describing an ecological framework for social relationships and support. The central tenet of the bioecological model is that a person's potential is encouraged through continuous exchanges labelled as proximal processes. These interactions balance protective and risk factors operating across multiple levels of the social ecology: at an intraindividual level, between the individual's physical and psychological characteristics (the microsystem); at a relational level, between the individual and significant others (the mesosystem); at an organisational level, by encompassing all formal structures of the society in which the individual is involved (the exosystem); and at a cultural level, due to the influence of prevailing values in a given space and time (the macrosystem) (Bronfenbrenner & Morris, 2006).

Many stories of world class athletes depict to perfection the interplay between proximal processes across the layers of reality proposed by the bio-ecological model, whether they are protective or not. Many of these athletes show intrinsic physical traits and a temperamental competitiveness to become world class competitors from an early age (microsystem). When they are interviewed, they sometimes remember how their attributes were dismissed by their parents. Most of them then go on to talk about how a coach or a mentor strongly encouraged them not to give up a sports career (mesosystem). Sometimes, this mentor helped to find a school that offered them optimal training conditions unavailable in their neighbourhood and convinced the parents to allow the child to move there, for classes and training. What these athletes never knew or often do not remember is that these new school's positive conditions (exosystem) were based on an ongoing national policy focused on supporting the development of young sports talents (macrosystem). This policy paid for local transportation from the child's neighbourhood to the school with these great training facilities.

Whether in the case of an outstanding athlete or of the common mortal, the proximal processes content is informed by the attributes of social entities in interaction, whether they are individuals or groups. According to the systems theory (Alarcão, 2000; Keller, 2005), these entities resemble complex systems. Complex systems are composites of sub-units or sub-systems, connected by a very large number of mutual and repeated exchanges also known as interactive patterns, which feedback and influence each sub-system (Alarcão, 2000). Social entities attributes parallel systems' characteristics that come to influence social relationships and support: they have the ability to spontaneously order themselves to achieve optimal or close to optimal functioning, according to their core values (*self-organisation*), tend towards balance in the face of small changes, striving for long periods of time (*robustness*); and are also prone to produce multiple and recursive interactions, in which the result of an interaction becomes a new input for the system (*feedback*). Moreover, two systems may achieve the same goal departing from distinct initial conditions or by following different paths (*unpredictability*) and its development depends on the reciprocity between the system itself and its environment, across time (*coevolution*). Furthermore, a complex system is more than the mere sum of its sub-systems, because it also includes its interactions (*totality*). Although complex systems are delimited by borders allowing them to be distinct entities, these borders are permeable, enabling a continuous interaction with other systems (*openness*). All these features of complex systems are integrated in an order whereby a system at one level is a sub-system or supra-system at another (*hierarchy*) (Alarcão, 2000; Keller, 2005).

Families are a classic example of a social entity reflecting complex system properties. They are social groups that connect a variable number of members (sub-systems) through continuous interactions, whether they occur on a daily basis (e.g. shared meals) or not (e.g. Christmas gatherings). These interactions reflect the family's core values, ranging from more traditional to more progressive ones (self-organisation), although these values may be incorporated or even rejected by the different members. Families are still among the most permanent social entities in Western societies, cutting across each of its member's different developmental stages, from childhood to retirement (robustness). However, family stability may be disturbed or even interrupted by unexpected life events (e.g. unemployment, sudden death) meaning that they are also subjected to unpredictability. Still, their robustness allows their members to mutually affect their development in areas such as learning or life decisions (coevolution). Moreover, family members are connected not only on the basis of each one's individuality but also considering the nature and quality of their members' ties (totality). Through their evolution, families are open to multiple influences of other systems, whether they are more tangible (e.g. neighbours) or distant (e.g. media). Furthermore, they can be categorised according to different criteria, such as origin (e.g. rural vs. urban) or socioeconomic status (hierarchy).

While proximal processes content is informed by complex systems attributes such as families, its structure can be mapped in the form of social networks. These correspond to all persons and interpersonal ties summed by a person (Keller & Blakeslee, 2013). Social networks are defined by their size (number of people included), density (the degree of interconnection between the network members), tie strength (reflected by the quality of the ties and support fulfilled by a certain connection), and the network composition (in terms of the members attributes, which may lead to more diverse or heterogeneous networks). Altogether, these network features may lead to the formation of cores of stronger and more permanent ties as the ones that, for instance, bring together a family, compared to cores which are less enduring, such as peer groups during adolescence (Varga & Zaff, 2017).

The organisation of social relationships across the multiple layers of the social ecology is fluid; changes to its content and structure occur across the different stages of the individual's life-span, which ultimately affect their efficacy. Adolescence, for instance, comprises important challenges to personal social interaction landscape. Adolescence is a long and dynamic transition between childhood and adulthood seeking for the definition of a personal identity. The accomplishment of this developmental task encompasses an increase and diversification of friendships, lesser centrality of parents, and greater openness to the influence of non-parental adults such as teachers and mentors (Cotterell, 2007; Smetana & Daddis, 2011). Altogether, these changes lead to a reconfiguration of social relationships, with implications for youths' development.

In an effort to better integrate the contributions of meta-models describing the content and structure of social interactions and youth development literature, Varga and Zaff (2017) propose the key notion of webs of support. Following the bioecological model perspective (Bronfenbrenner & Morris, 2006), these authors suggest that youth development is defined by the continuous relationship between a person and his/her contexts. The actualisation of human potential occurs within complex webs which integrate youth agency and characteristics, the relationships among all adults and peers in the web, the types of support these relationships provide, but also the distinct importance of each relationship for the individual. Thus, inside each core, some persons may be more important than others. The most relevant ties in each core are designated as anchors (Varga & Zaff, 2017). The coherence between youths' needs and the resources exchanged across social contexts and multiple relationships, especially across the relationships maintained with anchors, will lead to a supportive youth system that increases the probability of positive developmental outcomes.

The web of support approach sustains that the coherence or coordination between youths' anchors is essential for positive developmental pathways. This positioning goes beyond disperse theoretical and empirical findings acknowledging the need to integrate social ecological factors in youth mentoring theoretical models or the importance of the collaboration between mentors and anchor adults such as parents in shaping youth mentoring interactions (Keller, 2005; Simões & Alarcão, 2014; Spencer, Basualdo-Delmonico, & Lewis, 2011). By doing so, the web of support model also offers a rationale to overcome the idea that the links between youth mentoring and the wider framework of social relationships are fully described by the influence of the existing, and potential new ties of mentees' and mentors' social networks on the mentoring process and results and vice versa (Keller & Blakeslee, 2013). This idea establishes a theoretical background to assess how multiple social support coherence or coordination between anchors from different relational cores may actually contribute to youth development. The analysis of the impact of significant adults from different contexts is claimed for some time now (DuBois, Doolitle, Yates, Silverthorn, & Tebes, 2006). However, the support (dis)continuities delivered by these anchors remain understudied, because appropriate measurement models have not been developed (Varga & Zaff, 2017). It is this advancement which a MSSA perspective may add to the growing body of theoretical and empirical claims and findings linking youth mentoring to its social ecology.

Assessment trends in multiple social support and youth mentoring

Multiple social support in the youth development field of inquiry has been analysed from two predominant angles: *the unique or additive effects* approach and the *interactive effects approach*. The unique effects approach aggregates the majority of the studies in this domain of social developmental sciences by analysing the influence of each social support source on a given outcome, regardless of the effects of other social support sources (Larose et al., 2018;

Rueger, Malecki, & Demaray, 2010). According to this standpoint, a given source of support offers a unique contribution to youth development that the support from other adults cannot explain.

The comparison between the unique effects of multiple sources of support has covered youths' health, academic, or social outcomes, but has seldom included youth mentoring as a source of support. In the health domain, for instance, social support provided by family and friends (Cassarino-Perez & Dell'Aglio, 2015) or by mothers and partners (Pires, Araújo-Pedrosa, & Canavarro, 2014), has been linked to an improvement of quality-of-life prospects, respectively among clinically vulnerable youths and teenage mothers. Seemingly, lower levels of depression have been associated to the unique effect of family and friends (Patwardhan et al., 2017) or of parents, teachers, classmates, or friends (Rueger et al., 2010). Identical unique contributions of parents, peers, and teachers support have been found to predict lower youth social anxiety (Sahranc, Celik, & Turan, 2017). At least one study shows that natural mentors who provide inspiration for an academic or career path lead to youth life satisfaction above and beyond perceived support from parents and peers among disabled youths (Pham & Murray, 2016).

Youth positive academic outcomes have also been associated to the unique contribution of multiple sources of social support. For instance, Rueger et al. (2010) found that support delivered by parents and teachers leads to youths' more favourable attitudes towards school across boys and girls; however, classmates support is also decisive in backing more positive school attitudes in the case of boys. The same study depicts that parental support is less relevant for youths' academic adjustment compared to other adults' support, in later adolescence. Elsewhere, teacher support predicts youth academic adjustment (e.g. perceived academic competence, interest in academics, compliance with classroom norms) above and beyond perceptions of support from parents and family (Jiang, Huebner, & Siddall, 2013). At least one study (Farruggia, Bullen, & Davidson, 2013) shows that very important non-familial adults support is uniquely associated with the improvement of literacy and numeracy achievement among ethnically diverse youths', while parent and peer support warmth has no significant association with the same school achievement indicators.

Consistent with the unique or additive effects perspective, multiple social support has also been studied in association with youth positive social development outcomes. For instance, evidence shows that friends support has a unique greater impact in school and relational identity development compared to other sources (e.g. parents, teachers) (González, Cuéllar, Miguel, & Desfilis, 2009). Interestingly, the unique effects of youth mentoring on social development indicators compared to other adults unique influence on the same type of outcomes seems to be absent from the literature.

A second angle of multiple social support measurement which has spread more clearly in the mentoring literature focuses on the *interactive effects* between support sources (Larose et al., 2018). Interactive effects may follow two paths. First, mentor support can make a hierarchical compensatory contribution to youth development. In this case, the support provided by other sources (usually parents or teachers) interacts with mentor support in predicting youth adjustment. As an example of this model, Soucy and Larose (2000) found that in late adolescence, the associations between perceptions of mentoring support and college adjustment were stronger for youth with more secure maternal relationships.

Conversely, the hierarchical conditional model proposes that mentor support may also interact with other relationships support, but in a different way: the positive effect of mentor support may operate only if other support source is rewarding (Larose et al., 2018). This model of interactive effects is well documented by a study demonstrating that youth who perceive relationships with parents, peers, and teachers as satisfactory but not particularly strong benefit more from mentoring in terms of academic adjustment than do youth with profiles of either strongly positive or negative supportive relationships with these sources (Schwartz, Rhodes, Chan, & Herrera, 2011).

Multiple social support attunement: a brief definition

Two major gaps are evident in the literature focusing on the associations between multiple social support and youth development. A first one is specific of the youth mentoring research field, concerning the fact that mentors are not systematically considered as a key supportive source coming from the community in studies measuring unique effects associated with multiply sourced support. In part, this might be a side effect of the most outspread available measures of multiple social support, which do not include a scale to assess mentoring. However, and for the most part, the scarcity of unique effects reports including mentoring stem from a prevailing theoretical stand of considering mentors as adults who compensate for failed or adverse relationships such as inadequate parenting (Rhodes, 2002); this position has often lead to assessments describing interactive effects of youth mentoring with other relationships.

A second breach identified in the literature, and a major one affecting youth mentoring realm of research and multiple social support studies in general, is that perceived or enacted coherence between meaningful relationships or anchors from different cores has been ignored. Since 2015, a Portuguese research programme has addressed these gaps, by systematically integrating natural youth mentoring in the context of the examined multiple social support provided by anchor persons of different cores. The mentioned research programme has brought together complex systems theory and the web of support approaches (Varga & Zaff, 2017) with a new measurement approach labelled MSSA (Mendonça & Simões, 2019; Simões et al., 2018; Simões, Calheiros, Alarcão, Sousa, & Silva, 2018). Within this research programme, MSSA has been proposed as a complimentary assessment method to the measurement of youth social support according to unique/additive effects or interactive effects.

The definition of MSSA is rooted in the primitive meaning of the verb to attune. In a strict sense, to attune corresponds to bring into musical accord; in a broader sense, it refers to harmonise or adapt to a matter, action or idea (New Oxford Dictionary of English, 2012). The communal sense of attunement has been explored in psychological sciences in recent years. Erskine (1998) synthesises it as the ability of "going beyond empathy to enable a two-person experience of unbroken feeling connectedness, by providing a reciprocal affect and/or resonating a response" (p. 236). This sense of unity in relationships has grown as a reference to describe the formation of interpersonal contact unity in dyadic relationships, such as in psychotherapy (Erskine, 1998) or youth mentoring (Pryce, 2012). MSSA proposes a parallel use of the communion meaning of attunement, in terms of the degree of consistency or coordination across youths' anchors coming from different social cores, which may affect a given youth outcome (Simões et al., 2018).

In the youth multiple social support field, attunement is a twofold notion, because it addresses both multiple social support process, as well as its results. MSSA process refers to how the enacted coordination between multiple anchors from different social cores occurs, based on a lesser or greater intentionality of anchors to attune their support efforts. In MSSA enactment, anchors will act as sub-systems of their own systems or cores, through a multiple display of complex systems properties (Alarcão, 2000; Keller, 2005). Depending on the mobilisation of these properties, MSSA enactment may be classified according to three different stages aligned in a *continuum*:

- *Performance*: in this stage anchors show severe adherence to the values and interactive patterns of their core, minimising chances for MSSA coordination, especially when their supportive roles depart from very distinct sets of values.
- *Improvisation*: this may be described as a stage of MSSA whereby multiple anchors overlap their efforts, sometimes shifting away from the strict reproduction of their core's self-organised values and interactive patterns, while testing new strategies for support enactment. This attempt may lead to unintentional coordination, because anchors involved in youths' multiple social support can, at times, not be entirely aware of each other's supportive efforts. This unintentional coordination may be partial (when only the efforts of some of the regarded anchors display overlap) or total (when the efforts of all the regarded anchors overlap).
- *Rehearsal*: this stage corresponds to attempts in order to develop shared and coordinated positions between various youths' anchors where common experimental courses of action take place. In the process of experimenting, ways of joint collaboration are proposed, tested, and evaluated just as in a musical rehearsal.

One example can help to better identify different MSSA stages.

Jonathan is a 14-year-old boy at risk of school failure. He lives in a rural area, where school is not acknowledged as a means of social mobility. His father is a farmer and did not succeed at school. He appreciates Jonathan's help on the farm. An extra pair of hands is always welcomed. His class teacher is an experienced educator and has a long record of supporting students at risk of school failure. Over the years, she has earned the respect of other teachers and the school board in her quest to minimise this aspect. Jonathan is very close to Rob, a classmate who is one of the best students in class. Rob and his family have firm aspirations about Rob's education, as he wants to go to college.

In this case, at least three anchors from three different cores may display distinct MSSA configurations, ultimately affecting Jonathan's risk of school failure. MSSA would be organised as *performance* if Jonathan's father, teacher and classmate reproduced their core's standpoints, while enacting their specific social support to address his low school achievement situation. For instance, Jonathan's father could praise and motivate him to help on the farm, even if that meant less time to study. Meanwhile, his teacher would offer to tutor him, after classes, exactly when he should be helping on the farm. Moreover, Rob could be less available to help Jonathan with math, because he wanted to live up to his parents' expectations and improve in other subjects.

One can assume a different situation. In this scenario, Jonathan's father starts to encourage him to study math, while his class teacher insists on praising his effort in homework assignments and Rob convinces him that they could revise together immediately before each test. This scenario is brought forward without negotiation, with all of the implicated anchors moving towards total overlapping of their support efforts. This situation would correspond to a MSSA *total improvisation* stage. It could also happen that only Jonathan's class teacher and Rob showed non-negotiated efforts to help the young student improve his achievement. This would represent an example MSSA *partial improvisation*. Jonathan's case would reflect MSSA *rehearsal* stage if his anchors negotiated openly to have a common approach to social support enactment and strived to find common ground for their action.

The analysis of MSSA results is focused on how patterns of social support, organised in terms of the degree of perceived consistency between multiple anchors from distinct social cores, based on each anchor's support scores, will affect an outcome. Youths' intrapersonal patterns pertaining MSSA anchors may take one of at least three forms: *low-attuned multiple social support* involves low levels of perceived support from all anchors; *unattuned multiple social support* occurs when the level of perceived support is unbalanced across different anchors, with multiple combinations being possible; and *high-attuned multiple social support* occurs when all anchors offer perceived high levels of support (Simões et al., 2018).These patterns may then be studied as sources of youth development variation. Going back to Jonathan's case, the analysis

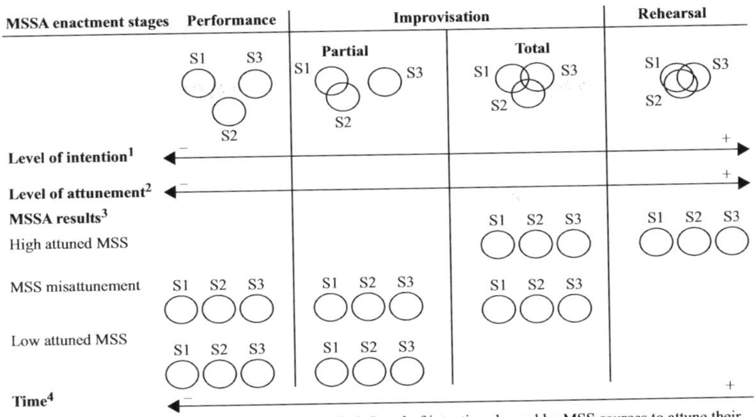

Legend: S1 – source 1; S2 – source 2; S3 – source 3; 1. Level of intention showed by MSS sources to attune their support efforts; 2. extent to which MSS sources display similar and/or agreed forms of support (graphically described by areas of overlap between SS sources); 3 Most likely MSSA results for respective enactment stage; 4. MSSA process and results are dyamic and may fluctuate across time.

Figure 6.1 Multiple social support attunement framework – graphical summary.

of MSSA results would focus on how he perceived his father, his teacher and his friend's levels of support and on how the support consistency across his anchors ultimately affected his school results.

Figure 6.1 offers a complete graphic display of MSSA and the most expected connections between MSSA enactment and MSSA results.

Multiple social support attunement and youth mentoring: preliminary findings

The following subsections summarise the results of the mentioned on-going Portuguese research project, which intends to untap the connections between MSSA patterns and youths' outcomes. These studies have analysed associations of multiple social support provided by parents, teachers, and natural mentors, with youths' social development as well as links between patterns of closer familial relationships, mentors, and best friends and youths' subjective well-being. These results are compared with prior parallel research when the same is available.

Multiple social support attunement and youth social development

One of the most noteworthy outcomes of youths' social support provided by anchors is the promotion of social development. Social development refers to the acquisition of social skills that enable children and youths to become members of families, peer groups, communities, or cultures (Killen & Coplan, 2011). The influence of the consistency between the support delivered by adult anchors, namely among parents, teachers, and natural mentors, and its effects on youths' social development has not merited a comprehensive attention from researchers. Two studies integrated in the stated research programme aimed at tackling this shortcoming. One explored how support attunement between parents, teachers, and mentors related to five 818 rural early adolescents' ($M = 12.15$; $SD = .81$; 54.2% girls) prosocial behaviour, self-regulation, antisocial behaviour, alcohol use, and 1-year substance use intention (Samos et al., 2018). Considering that these youths were in the transition to adolescence, the option was to assess youths' perceptions about anchors' autonomy support. The anchors were selected by the participants based on their opinion about who was the most important figure in setting norms and rules in the family (father, mother, or other) and in school (most influential teacher in this area). Mentors were targeted as the most important non-familial adult with who the youths met at least once a week for more than 12 months. At the same time, this study compared the total amount of support delivered by these anchor adults with the consistency of support among them in connecting with youths' social development. Three central findings emerged from the study, after controlling for the effect of the participants' age. First, using a cluster analysis approach, a four-group cluster solution in terms of the combination of the parents, teachers, and mentors perceived support was the most accurate and interpretable. Two groups gathered similar support perceptions across the three sources of support (one classified as low attuned multiple autonomy support attunement and the other as high attuned multiple autonomy support attunement). Others, however, depicted unattuned patterns of support, one due to low rates of parent autonomy support and the other due to low rates of teacher autonomy support, when compared to the remaining sources. Second, a pattern of perceived high attuned support among parent, teacher, and natural mentor delivered better prospects for youth's prosocial behaviour and self-regulation, as opposed to high levels of perceived total support offered by the same anchor adults. Finally, a cluster of low teacher autonomy support (as opposed to high attunement among parent and mentor) delivered the worst prospects on the selected indicators of social development.

A second study involving 645 rural early adolescents ($M = 12.30$; $SD = .60$; 55.35% girls) tested if the connections between autonomy support attunement and youths' antisocial behaviour, prosocial behaviour, and self-regulation would be different across different socioeconomic (SES) levels. Through latent class analysis, four different patterns of perceived social support attunement between anchors were found, but only one of the patterns depicted unbalanced perceived support, based on teachers' low autonomy support. Subsequent analysis demonstrated that the associations between autonomy support attunement and the social development indicators were not distinct across different SES levels. Moreover, highly consistent support between parent, most important teacher, and natural mentor was associated with all the selected social development indicators, irrespectively of youths' SES (Simões et al., 2018).

Multiple social support attunement and youths' subjective well-being

The connections between MSSA and youths' development in terms of their well-being are insufficiently studied. At least two studies in a recent past have reported some relevant findings. For instance, Levitt et al. (2005) found that patterns of high-attuned social support from close family and friends were linked to fewer internalisation problems (including depression and anxiety) among early adolescents. The same trend was found among older lesbian, gay, bisexual, and transgender youths receiving consistently high support from family, friends, and significant others (McConnell, Birkett, & Mustanski, 2015).

The research programme here summarised also looked at how consistency of support among anchor relationships from three cores, family, community, and friendships, would relate with 236 disadvantaged youths' ($M = 14.10$; $SD = 1.78$; 60.20% boys) subjective well-being, measured in terms of quality-of-life, depression, and social anxiety (Mendonça & Simões, 2019). Again, the analysis involved anchor relationships, namely the closest family member, the natural mentor, and best friend. High attuned MSSA proved to be an optimal pattern to promote these youths' subjective well-being in terms of greater quality-of-life, lower social anxiety, and lower depression among disadvantaged youths. These results are coherent with prior reports (e.g. McConnell et al., 2015), showing that greater MSSA contributes to improved adjustment. In this case, the connections between high MSSA and subjective well-being indicators were also more generalised, systematic, and greater than the ones found between gender or age and the same subjective well-being indicators.

A multiple social support attunement framework for youth mentoring research: roads to be travelled

The research programme focused on the links between MSSA and youth development summarised above is a collection of exploratory studies. Moreover, the available studies have focused on potential results delivered by MSSA, but have not investigated MSSA processes yet. This means that there are several questions resulting from a MSSA framework for youth mentoring. A non-exhaustive systematisation of these questions according to the web of support model key premises (Varga & Zaff, 2017) can help to set new paths for research.

According to the web of support model, youth agency shapes social support of both weak and strong ties in youths' social network. Thus, social support is a bidirectional process, affecting social support availability and judgements about enacted and perceived MSSA. The attunement between youths' needs and youth mentors support (Pryce, 2012) and how this communion can help to improve relationships with other anchors (e.g. parents) has been highlighted by some reports (e.g. Spencer et al., 2011). A MSSA standpoint may contribute to understand if dyadic attunement within mentoring is relevant to improve enacted as well as perceived MSSA among the mentee's anchors.

The web of support relies on the consideration of youths whole social ecology as sources of influence of youth development. A systemic approach has addressed the need to understand if youth mentoring is influenced and/or may reshape youths' social networks in terms of dimension, distribution, or density, as well as the social resources or social capital resulting from those potential changes (Keller & Blakeslee, 2013). A MSSA framework may add to this broader picture of youth mentoring interactions within the social ecology by enabling to understand how MSSA enactment occurs and if it fits the suggested framework of MSSA stages (performance, improvisation, and rehearsal). It may also inform if different stages of MSSA enactment influence the relational intensity and configuration of mentees' social network and social capital changes.

The remaining web of support premises emphasise the plasticity of youth social support. On one hand, different anchors provide different types of support which may interact between each other. On the other hand, youth support needs and configurations change across time (Varga & Zaff, 2017). This evolutive nature of multiple social support across social cores and time leads to different research implications. One implication would be to determine the turning points that increase multiple anchors chances to switch from a given MSSA stage of enactment (e.g. performance) to another (e.g. rehearsal). Considering that the optimal MSSA for youth development seems to be the one in which greater attunement among anchors is achieved (Mendonça & Simões, 2019; Simões et al., 2018), pinpointing the critical moments or actions leading to greater coordination chances seems warranted. In addition, the identification of those turning points would represent a major contribution to the MSSA research and youth mentoring literature, if they could be described according to youths' specific needs or stressors, facilitating its management by programme coordinators and improving support deliverance. Finally, until now, MSSA research has stand as a collection of snapshots of meaningful patterns between youth anchor relationships in a given moment. Anchors' influence on mentoring and vice versa vary significantly form early adolescence to young adulthood. Longitudinal studies may help to specify developmental moments when mentors may be more influential to improve enacted and perceived attunement across meaningful anchors or if mentoring can leverage support deliverance across anchors in particularly stressful moments such as developmental transitions (Cotterell, 2007).

Given the exploratory path of research completed until now, it is certainly a risk to pinpoint solid practical implications of MSSA research for youth mentoring. More consistent research efforts, based on qualitative and longitudinal designs may document some potential breakthroughs for youth mentoring practice suggested by existing research. Nevertheless, these may be organised in, at least, three core features of youth mentoring. A MSSA perspective may lead formal mentoring programmes to incorporate anchors' attunement as a programme goal. Further research may unveil the developmental moments and situations in which that may seem a desirable aim. Finally, a MSSA approach may help to unveil when attunement is required or useful between mentors and other anchors or when mentors are required to compensate for prior unsuccessful relationships with other meaningful relationships (Spencer et al., 2011).

A MSSA framework underlines the role of high MSSA in improving positive social development and well-being among adolescents. This central result may inspire youth policy decision-making in two different ways. First, youth services deliverance may need to develop interventions that improve the connections and attunement between anchors of different cores. This approach may be particularly relevant for those working in community settings or using (multi)systemic therapeutic approaches, which are often challenged by the need to adjust the efforts of different sources of support. Second, these results show the need to better assess and implicate MSSA in programmes and interventions across different sectors of public and private formal support providers. These providers, situated at the exosystem level (Bronfenbrenner & Morris, 2006), tend to focus on relevant support providers in their domain. For instance, a health service provider may be overly focused on how parental involvement prevents adolescents' alcohol consumption. However, the attunement of adolescents' best friends or community-based mentors' support may strengthen the targeted outcome.

References

Alarcão, M. (2000). *Desequilíbrios familiares* [Family (un)balance]. Coimbra: Quarteto Editora.

Bronfenbrenner, U., & Morris, P. A. (2006). The bioecological model of human development. In R. M. Lerner, & W. Damon (Eds.), *Handbook of child psychology: Theoretical models of human development* (pp. 793–828). Hoboken, NJ: John Wiley & Sons Inc.

Cassarino-Perez, L., & Dell'Aglio, D. D. (2015). Processos de resiliência em adolescentes com diabetes Melitus tipo I [Resilience processes in adolescents with Melitus diabetes type I]. *Psicologia em Estudo, 20*(1), 45–56. https://doi.org/10.4025/psicolestud.v20i1.24035.

Cotterell, J. (2007). *Social networks in youth and adolescence*. New York, NY: Routledge.

DuBois, D. L., Doolittle, F., Yates, B. T., Silverthorn, N., & Tebes, J. K. (2006). Research methodology and youth mentoring. *Journal of Community Psychology, 34*(6), 657–676. https://doi.org/10.1002/jcop.20122

DuBois, D. L., Portillo, N., Rhodes, J. E., Silverthorn, N., & Valentine, J. C. (2011). How effective are mentoring programs for youth? A systematic assessment of the evidence. *Psychological Science in the Public Interest, Supplement, 12*(2), 57–91. https://doi.org/10.1177/1529100611414806

Erskine, R. (1998). Attunement and involvement: Therapeutic responses to relational needs. *International Journal of Psychotherapy, 3*(3), 235–244.

Farruggia, S. P., Bullen, P., & Davidson, J. (2013). Important nonparental adults as an academic resource for youth. *Journal of Early Adolescence, 33*(4), 498–522. https://doi.org/10.1177/0272431612450950

González, J. J., Cuéllar, A., Miguel, J. M., & Desfilis, E. (2009). El desarrollo de la identidad en la adolescencia y adultez emergente: Una comparación de la identidad global frente a la identidad en dominios específicos [Identity development in adolescence e young adulthood: A comparison between general identity and specific identity dimensions]. *Anales de Psicologia, 25*(2), 316–329.

Jiang, X., Huebner, E. S., & Siddall, J. (2013). A short-term longitudinal study of differential sources of school-related social support and adolescents' school satisfaction. *Social Indicators Research, 114*, 1073–1086. https://doi.org/10.1007/s11205-012-0190-x.

Keller, T. E. (2005). A systemic model of the youth mentoring intervention. *Journal of Primary Prevention, 26*(2), 169–188. https://doi.org/10.1007/s10935-005-1850-2

Keller, T. E., & Blakeslee, J. E. (2013). Social networks and mentoring. In *Handbook of youth mentoring* (pp. 129–142). New York, NY: SAGE Publications Inc. https://doi.org/10.4135/9781412996907.n9

Killen, M., & Coplan, R. J. (2011). Social development: Concepts, theory, and overview. In M. Killen, & R. J. Coplan (Eds.), *Social development in childhood and adolescence* (pp. 3–11). Oxford, UK: Wiley-Blackwell.

Larose, S., Boisclair-Châteauvert, G., De Wit, D. J., DuBois, D., Erdem, G., & Lipman, E. L. (2018). How mentor support interacts with mother and teacher support in predicting youth academic adjustment: An investigation among youth exposed to Big Brothers Big Sisters of Canada Programs. *Journal of Primary Prevention, 39*, 205–228. https://doi.org/10.1007/s10935-018-0509-8

McConnell, E. A., Birkett, M. A., & Mustanski, B. (2015). Typologies of social support and associations with mental health outcomes among LGBT youth. *LGBT Health, 2*(1), 55–61. https://doi.org/10.1089/lgbt.2014.0051

Mendonça, C., & Simões, F. (2019). Disadvantaged youths' subjective well-being: The role of gender, age, and multiple social support attunement. *Child Indicators Research, 12*(3), 769–789. https://doi.org/10.1007/s12187-018-9554-3

Patwardhan, I., Mason, W. A., Savolainen, J., Chmelka, M. B., Miettunen, J., & Järvelin, M. R. (2017). Childhood cumulative contextual risk and depression diagnosis among young adults: The mediating roles of adolescent alcohol use and perceived social support. *Journal of Adolescence, 60*, 16–26. https://doi.org/10.1016/j.adolescence.2017.07.008.

Pham, Y. K., & Murray, C. (2016). Social relationships among adolescents with disabilities: Unique and cumulative associations with adjustment. *Exceptional Children, 82*, 234–250.

Pires, R., Araújo-Pedrosa, A., & Canavarro, M. C. (2014). Examining the links between perceived impact of pregnancy, depressive symptoms, and quality of life during adolescent pregnancy: The buffering role of social support. *Maternal and Child Health Journal, 18*(4), 789–800. https://doi.org/10.1007/s10995-013-1303-0.

Pryce, J. (2012). Mentor attunement: An approach to successful school-based mentoring relationships. *Child and Adolescent Social Work Journal, 29*(4), 285–305. http://doi.org/10.1007/s10560-012-0260-6

Rueger, S. Y., Malecki, C. K., & Demaray, M. K. (2010). Relationship between multiple sources of perceived social support and psychological and academic adjustment in early adolescence: Comparisons across gender. *Journal of Youth and Adolescence, 39*(1), 47–61. http://doi.org/10.1007/s10964-008-9368-6

Sahranc, U., Celik, E., & Turan, M. (2017). Mediating and moderating effects of social support in the relationship between social anxiety and hope levels in children. *Journal of Happiness Studies*, 1–17. https://doi.org/10.1007/s10902-017-9855-0.

Sarason, I. G., & Sarason, B. R. (2009). Social support: Mapping the construct. *Journal of Social and Personal Relationships, 26*, 113–120. https://doi.org/10.1177/0265407509105526.

Schwartz, S. E. O., Rhodes, J. E., Chan, C. S., & Herrera, C. (2011). The impact of school-based mentoring on youths with different relational profiles. *Developmental Psychology, 47*(2), 450–462. https://doi.org/10.1037/a0021379

Simões, F., & Alarcão, M. (2014). Promoting well-being in school-based mentoring through basic psychological needs support: Does it really count? *Journal of Happiness Studies, 15*, 407–424. https://doi.org/10.1007/s10902-013-9428-9

Simões, F., Calheiros, M., & Alarcão, M. (2018). Socioeconomic status, multiple social support attunement and early adolescents' social development, *Journal of Community Psychology, 46*(6), 790–805. https://doi.org/10.1002/jcop.21973

Simões, F., Calheiros, M., Alarcão, M., Sousa, A., & Silva, O. (2018). Total and attuned autonomy support and early adolescents' social development. *Journal of Child and Family Studies, 27*(2), 374–386. https://doi.org/10.1007/s10826-017-0911-5

Smetana, J. G., & Daddis, C. (2011). Domain-specific antecedents of parental psychological control and monitoring: The role of parenting beliefs and practices. In M. Killen, & R. J. Coplan (Eds.), *Social development in childhood and adolescence: A contemporary reader*. Malden: Wiley-Blackwell.

Soucy, N., & Larose, S. (2000). Attachment and control in family and mentoring contexts as determinants of adolescent adjustment at college. *Journal of Family Psychology, 14*(1), 125–143. https://doi.org/10.1037/0893-3200.14.1.125

Spencer, R., Basualdo-Delmonico, A., & Lewis, T. O. (2011). Working to make it work: The role of parents in the youth mentoring process. *Journal of Community Psychology, 39*(1), 51–59. https://doi.org/10.002/jcop20416

Varga, S. M., & Zaff, J. F. (2017). Webs of support: An integrative framework of relationships, social networks, and social support for positive youth development. Adolescent Research Review. Retrieved from https://doi.org/10.1007/s40894-017-0076-x

Chapter 7

The methodological issues in the assessment of quality and the benefits of formal youth mentoring interventions

The case of the Czech Big Brothers Big Sisters/Pět P

Tereza Brumovská and Gabriela Seidlová Málková

This chapter aims to discuss the evolution of methodology on assessing the quality and benefits of formal youth mentoring interventions. We argue that the research and praxis of youth mentoring programmes currently need to implement more qualitative research methods to gain an in-depth understanding of the principles of mentoring and the relational features that mediate its benefits.

We understand mentoring in this text as a social phenomenon that naturally exists in human social networks. We think that beneficial youth mentoring interventions should aim to facilitate relationships in the qualities of natural mentoring, to achieve the benefits of formal mentoring for children and young people. Thus, first in this chapter, we focus on identifying what we recognise as the quality features of the natural mentoring relationship (NMR). We also show that the link between natural mentoring and formal youth mentoring interventions is elaborated in the Mentoring Process Model (Rhodes, 2005).

Later in the text, we discuss research methods used in current mentoring literature and the efficacy of these on how to develop high standards for quality mentoring social and support services within a given educational or social context. We particularly argue that the currently available research evaluations generally underestimate the role of the theoretical rationale and, as a result, they lose the "interpretive" power to understand manifestations of relational quality and the perceived benefits of mentoring interventions.

Finally, using a brief review of studies conducted by the authors of this chapter on the Czech mentoring programme Big Brothers Big Sisters/Pět P between 2004 and 2017, we propose the qualitative "interpretive perspective" as a promising methodological approach for addressing the gaps in current knowledge in the field of youth mentoring.

The phenomena of natural mentoring and its link to formal youth mentoring research

A NMR is a mutual caring connection between an older, wiser, caring mentor, and a younger, less-experienced mentee that can be formed and developed spontaneously at any time during the lifespan. NMRs have been part of our organic social networks. They are observable as human relationships that have been developed over generations throughout history (Freedman, 1992). The first use of the word "Mentor" is in Homer's *Odyssey*.[1] An NMR is one where someone gains new knowledge, support, and personal development as a result of the bond (Bennetts, 2003). It facilitates social learning, where the mentee acquires a particular set of skills, values, and practices (Blinn-Pike, 2007; Rogoff, 1990), higher resiliency in risk behaviour, development in social relationships and improved attitudes to school and education as well as a sense of well-being and health as a result of a mentoring bond (DuBois & Silverthorn, 2005; Rhodes, Contreras, & Mangelsdorf, 1994; Sánchez, Esparza, Berardi, & Pryce, 2011; Werner & Smith, 2001; Zimmerman, Bingerheimer, & Notaro, 2002). An NMR is characterised by mutual respect, loyalty and an interest in facilitating social, emotional, and cognitive learning that affects positively on the mentees' development (DuBois & Silverthorn, 2005; Rhodes, Contreras, & Mangelsdorf, 1994; Sánchez, Esparza, Berardi, & Pryce, 2011; Werner & Smith, 2001; Zimmerman, Bingerheimer, & Notaro, 2002). As well as forming a secure emotional bond with a mentee, the mentor offers models of behaviour, values, attitudes and practical, problem-solving skills. They offer social support that gives mentees opportunities to learn and develop talents and abilities (DuBois & Silverthorn, 2005; Rhodes, Contreras, & Mangelsdorf, 1994; Sánchez, Esparza, Berardi, & Pryce, 2011; Van Dam et al., 2018; Werner & Smith, 2001; Zimmerman, Bingerheimer, & Notaro, 2002).

Thus, mentors facilitate mentees' social and emotional growth and the development of children's competence and autonomy (Brumovská & Seidlová Málková, 2010; Cutrona, 2000; Dolan & Brady, 2012; Ryan & Solky, 1996). Natural mentors are most often grandparents, uncles, aunts, neighbours, parents of a boy- or girlfriends, youth leaders, or members of church groups (Werner & Smith, 2001). More in-depth studies on natural mentoring processes and principles that mediate mentoring benefits in children and youths' development are yet to be conducted to fill the gap in the current literature. The occurrence of natural mentoring and its perceived benefits among children and young people in Europe have notably not yet been explored in depth (Brumovská, 2017; Rhodes, 2018).

To some extent, we can understand how a theory of mediated learning proposed by Vygotsky (1978) and later elaborated by Feuerstein, Yaacov and Rynders (1988) into a mediated learning experience theory is linked to youth mentoring as a theoretical framework for explaining principles and the importance of natural mentoring. However, both Vygotsky and Feuerstein primarily emphasise the role of the social interaction of an intentioned adult and a child from the perspective of learning processes and cognitive skills development. The mentoring research, on the other hand, seeks specifications of how natural mentoring (the frame and the space for mediated learning) is supported in different social settings of current societies to enable the positive cognitive, socio-emotional, and individual development of a mentee (Brumovská, 2017).

Following the observation of benefits of NMR, Rhodes (2005), from the outset of research literature in the field of youth mentoring, proposed the first theoretical model on helping processes in formal mentoring relationships. This model, called Pathways of Benefits in FYMRs (Rhodes, 2005) identifies key features of mentoring that create conditions that are beneficial for children and youths. Rhodes developed the model on a strong background of social-psychological theories, mentoring research at the time, as well as on the observation of NMR in her professional practice. She argues that mentoring has a positive impact on a mentee's socio-emotional, cognitive, and identity development. Her model distinguishes casual, moderating and mediating aspects, and social actors. She was the first author who included relevant social actors and their influence on the benefits of FYMRs on mentees' development.

What is of great importance in Rhodes's model is the identification of the relational features that predict the quality of mentor-mentee relational characteristics. These identified features – the experiences of closeness, trust, and empathy – indeed mediate the benefits (positive results) of NMR and in formal mentoring relationships, if thrived (see also Brumovska, Seidlová Málková, in print for further discussion). Rhodes's model is essential in the development of praxis in formal youth mentoring interventions as it introduces and applies the principles and benefits of natural mentoring in formal youth mentoring relationships.

The problem of evaluating efficacy in formal youth mentoring interventions

NMR are claimed to be vulnerable or even malfunctioning in societies with postmodern family systems (Beck, 1992; De Singly, 1999; Freedman, 1992). Formal youth mentoring interventions have thus been used as prevention and early intervention services for socially disadvantaged children and young people across Europe and the United States. In recent decades, they have gained popularity in the praxis of social and educational services and attracted the attention of social sciences researchers (Brumovská & Seidlová Málková, 2010; Dolan & Brady, 2012; Hall, 2003).

Formal youth mentoring interventions, where socially disadvantaged children and young people benefit from quality interactions and relationships with volunteer mentors, aim to foster the roles and qualities of (missing) natural mentors. In other words, theoretically, characteristics, qualities, and benefits of NMR are systematically implemented in a professional social/educational framework to subsidise deficits in NMR (Brumovská, 2017; Brumovská & Seidlová Málková, 2010). Research studies conducted to date, however, showed that formal mentoring relationships are not automatically beneficial for mentees, they need to be carefully organised and in certain circumstances can be harmful to mentees (Brumovská, 2017; Colley, 2003; Grossman & Rhodes, 2002; Morrow & Styles, 1995, 1992; Spencer, 2007). Thus, there still is a need for more research on effective strategies to implement natural mentoring principles into professional social/educational intervention systems.

The so-called "positivist paradigm" is characterised by a firm belief in the existence of an external, physical reality guided by underlying laws, and by a conviction that knowledge of this reality can be uncovered using correct scientific methods (Clarke, 2009). The positivist perspective originates in the natural sciences, where it typically concentrates on discovering underlying causal principles (Javornicky, 2018). Research and evaluation studies of formal youth mentoring interventions rooted in evidence-based approaches typically use methodology tightly linked to cause and effect, experimental principles using positivist views on the research problems. The critical issue in this approach is a theoretical claim (hypotheses) relating mentoring implementation to improvements at the level of children's (risk) behaviours and social relationships. Of course, the "theoretical" presumptions creating the baseline for experimental intervention studies are of crucial importance here. The more general the hypotheses would be, the more vague or particular the results we should expect.

Mentoring relationship literature and praxis seem to traditionally believe in the "corrective" impact of mentoring on children and young people. In other words, research in the field of mentoring relationships traditionally focused on proving the corrective effects of mentoring interventions on young people's identified deficits and anti-social behaviours (Brady & O'Regan, 2009; Brumovská & Málková, 2010; Colley, 2003; Philip, 1997). The methodology used to explore these possible causal relations should then have the capacity to prove the existence, strength, or importance of these theorised relations.

Besides, various experimental and quasi-experimental studies of the outcomes of mentoring interventions share the presumption that mentoring functions as a stress and risk buffer and thus as a protective factor in children's resilience (Brady & O'Regan, 2009; Dolan et al., 2010). Evaluations, therefore, focus on measures in children's and young people's perceptions of social supports and in their resiliency and well-being, comparing these before and after their experiences in the mentoring programmes.

Randomised Control Trial (RCT) design is one example of a preferred experimental methodology in this regard. For instance, the major RCT study carried out on probably the most popular and researched mentoring programme, the Big Brothers Big Sisters (BBBS) programme by Public/Private Ventures in the United States (Tierney et al., 1997) studied the impact of mentoring on young people in terms of positive changes in mentees' antisocial and risk behaviours. It concluded that youths with a mentor were less likely to hit someone or to start using drugs or alcohol, had better school attendance and results, had improved attitudes to completing schooling and education, and had improved relationships with family and peers than control-group youths with the same issues. Results of this study served as essential guidance in decisions at the level of social policy on the implementation of youth mentoring interventions in the United States. At the same time, RCT research designs in a real setting are known to be challenging to implement, time-consuming, and costly (Kraemer, 2015), and are under the source of constant discussion regarding its ethical and methodological difficulties (Brady & O'Regan, 2009).

Another significant mixed-method evaluation study was carried out in Ireland (Dolan et al., 2010, 2011). Its methodology is based on the widely accepted Rhodes "mentoring process" model (Rhodes, 2005). This major RCT study was completed with semi-structured interviews led in the dialectic approach to the experimental design, arguing for the analysis of mixed data arising from the different epistemologies (Brady & O'Regan, 2009; Dolan et al., 2010, 2011). However, the depth of its qualitative methodology was limited by the semi-structured interviews designed to complete the major survey done in the positivist cause-effect approach. Moreover, Rhodes' theoretical model that provided a framework to the qualitative part of the study does not explain the internal processes in mentoring relationships, in which the relational quality features and thus the mentoring benefits are developed (Brumovská, 2017; Brumovská & Seidlová Málková, 2020).

Two widely cited meta-analytical studies on the effectiveness of formal mentoring programmes and intervention were conducted (DuBois et al., 2002, 2011). Both studies together analysed reports and research outcomes published between 1975 and 2010 (approximately 120 in total, including 73 studies conducted in experimental and quasi-experimental designs). In respect to the effectiveness of the mentoring intervention, the authors concluded that gains on outcome measures for the typical mentoring programmes users were rather modest (DuBois et al., 2011). The positive impact of mentoring was identified in the areas of enhanced psychological, social, academic, and job/employment functioning and in reducing risk behaviours (DuBois et al., 2011).

It needs to be stressed that the positive effects and meaningfulness of implementing mentoring programmes was proven in international literature. At the same time, it needs to be emphasised that experimental and RCT designs have difficulty capturing the mentoring relational dynamics and processes and the quality of experience in these features that mediate the benefits of mentoring relationships (Brumovská & Seidlová Málková, 2010; Morrow & Styles, 1995; Rhodes, 2005). The experimental approach to mentoring evaluations is feasible for the field while using the theories of social supports and risk and resiliency as the explanation of mentoring effects. However, these theoretical frameworks and related research studies do not explore the in-depth mentoring processes that mediate mentoring benefits. As a result, the principles that mediate the benefits of youth mentoring to children and causing a positive impact of mentoring interventions on young people remain theoretically and empirically unclear in the literature to date (Brumovská, 2017; Brumovská & Seidlová Málková, 2010; Zand et al., 2009).

In sum, we argue that the future research on mentoring should concentrate more on the fact that mentoring is a positive experience that can support mentees' development in a positive way (Brumovská & Seidlová Málková, 2010). The focus of mentoring programmes, their evaluation and mentoring research should thus be on exploring mentoring relationships and their qualities that foster the characteristics and benefits of natural mentoring. We understand this shift towards the qualitative interpretive perspectives in research on examining and evaluating mentoring phenomena, their experiences and perceived benefits as logical research progress in the field.

The framework of the interpretive perspective (Creswell, 2013) assumes that there is a difference between an objective reality of physical objects "out there" – subjected to natural forces and measured with an experimental research design – and the socially constructed systems of relationships that exist between humans in society. In this worldview, socially constructed knowledge mediates the understanding of the phenomena in the social world (Creswell, 2013). The researcher's task is to seek to understand and interpret social reality in terms of this socially constructed knowledge. Thus, the interpretive paradigm gives value to individuals' voices and their experiences with the given social phenomena (Smith et al., 2012).

The goal of research in this perspective is to explore the subjectivity of experiences and meanings in their historical context of people's culture and society (Creswell, 2013, p. 23). In other words, it seeks an understanding of people's living world and their experience with particular phenomena. It addresses the interactions between people and explores the subjective meanings of experiences to understand phenomena in their complexity (Creswell, 2013; Smith et al., 2012). The researcher thus aims to interpret people's experience of phenomena and the context that shapes those experiences, to understand what meanings the phenomena have for people. The research inquiry is generated inductively to develop theory or patterns of meaning in subjective experiences (Creswell, 2013, pp. 23–25).

We think that mentoring should be understood as a complex social phenomenon (Brumovska, 2017) and as such it should be mainly explored as an experience of individuals and its characteristics, qualities, and perceived benefits in mentoring relationships, rather than as the outcomes of mentoring and its causal impact on children's development. The interpretive paradigm is, therefore viable for such exploration and assessment. We argue that as far as the mentoring relationship itself creates a positive and satisfying experience for its recipients – and if its experiences, characteristics and benefits are explored as experience of mentoring as social phenomena – the outcomes expected in the causal model of experimental evaluation are inherently present as a result of this positive experience of mentoring (Brumovská, 2017; Brumovska & Seidlova Malkova, 2020).

An example of the practical use of the interpretative paradigm in research is an Interpretive Phenomenological Analysis, IPA (Smith et al., 2012). We understand it as an especially suitable and promising methodology for future research exploring mentoring experiences and benefits (see Brumovská, 2017). Implementing IPA methodology opens up the possibility to broaden and enhance theoretical knowledge about the essential principles of the quality of mentoring programmes, the quality of mentoring experience, and the nature of mentoring relationships itself.

The next section aims to show – on the case of research conducted on cohorts of Czech participants – how the interpretive, qualitative approach to mentoring research saturates the evaluation of the quality of mentoring relationships in formal youth mentoring interventions. The section is based on research conducted between 2004 and 2017. We try to show here how we came to an appreciation of the use of IPA methodology in the research on the efficacy of youth mentoring programmes in the Czech social-educational system.

We particularly outline the development of research methods in the studies on youth mentoring we conducted, starting with the survey questionnaires in 2003 and moving through content analysis on mentoring roles to the application of a qualitative longitudinal IPA study on mentoring experience and its characteristics and quality in 2017. We mention how we approached the research evaluation on the impact of the Czech Big Brothers Big Sisters/Pět P in 2003, assessing the survey questionnaires used by the programme as an evaluation tool at the time. The conclusions of this first study were then further developed in the two qualitative explorative studies on characteristics of mentors´ approach to children in mentoring relationships (Brumovská, 2007; Brumovská & Seidlová Málková, 2008). Finally, these Czech research studies were completed with the longitudinal qualitative study on the features, quality and dynamics of formal youth mentoring relationships (Brumovská, 2017), using the interpretive phenomenological analysis (Smith et al., 2012).

A brief review of research conducted in the Czech mentoring intervention programme

Generally speaking, we conducted four major studies between 2004 and 2017 on the efficacy of a Czech version of the BBBS mentoring programme, called "Pět P" (Brumovská, 2017, 2009, 2003[2]; Brumovská & Málková, 2010, 2008).

BBBS CZ/Programme Pět P was the most extensive mentoring intervention in the Czech Republic at the time our research started. Its operation was implemented in 1996 in Prague and was based on the methods of the Big Brothers Big Sisters of America programme. The BBBS CZ programme operated through approximately 20 affiliates that were part of different statutory and voluntary organisations, but mainly under Voluntary Centres (civic associations for promoting volunteering and civic engagement in society) or SVP – statutory Centres for Special Education, Support, and Care that aim to provide services to disadvantaged children and families in prevention and early intervention services. Affiliates of BBBS CZ recruited, trained, matched, and supervised voluntary mentors in line with the practices of BBBS International to develop mentoring matches. Volunteers, children and parents in BBBS CZ agreed to be involved and to support regular one-to-one mentoring meetings for at least 10 months. The BBBS CZ affiliate in Prague took part in the research studies.

Mentors are volunteers who can be seen by the mentoring programme in different roles relative to the programme's mission, aims, and objectives (Frič & Pospíšilová, 2010). The BBBS CZ affiliate in Prague trained mentors mainly as agents of change in civil society (Frič & Pospíšilová, 2010) through their volunteering activity in the programme. The programme was based generally on the idea that a mentor is a volunteer, non-professionally and informally related to the child, and function as a friend and role model. Mentors dedicate time and interest to the child, spending enjoyable time together once a week and gaining good experiences and joy from their meetings. The mentors benefit from the relationship and the programme setting as well as the child, which motivates mentors to volunteer (Programme Pět P Manual for Caseworkers, 2007).

Mentors should have no particular goal in the relationship except to develop an enjoyable, friendly relationship and spend time with the child in mutually agreeable activities once a week, over at least 10 months (Brumovská & Seidlová Málková, 2010). The approach of a mentor thus depended more on their personality and the perception of the child and their needs, as well as the mentor's motivation for the relationship. Mentors, in the beginning, had to find a connection with the child, which established a close mutual relationship. They had to discover their role in the relationship, which was suitable for the child's needs as well as enjoyable and satisfying for themselves so that they could stay involved long-term (Brumovská & Málková, 2008; Programme Pět P Manual for Caseworkers, 2007).

The first Czech study was conducted as a part of the bachelor research thesis assessing the viability of the survey at the time frequently used as a tool for evaluation of the BBBS mentoring programme efficacy (Programme-Based Outcome Evaluation, POE). The study aimed to explore the strengths of the Czech BBBS programme.

POE was originally developed in the United States, following the results of Tierney's (1997) RCT study and then adopted in 1999 as a method of evaluating the Czech BBBS CZ programme in translation from the English version. POE consisted of survey questionnaires to assess the changes in children mainly by mentors. There were 18 questions in three main domains (Trust, Skills, and Relationships). The survey asked mentors to assess the efficacy of their impact on mentees (Brumovská, 2003).

The study concluded that self-assessment of the effectiveness in the mentoring role, by the mentor him or herself, can be highly biased. Mentors probably tend to reflect their mentoring efficiency in a way that gives a definite meaning to their involvement (Brumovská, 2003; Brumovská & Seidlová Málková, 2008). The study also concluded that evaluating the direct experience and perceived benefits of mentoring participants in the mentoring relationships would be a more accurate method to assess changes in children's behaviour, rather than using the questionnaires assessed by mentoring participants.

As a result, the "POE study" recommended the use of in-depth qualitative interviews with mentoring actors – mentors in particular – on the approach to children in the mentoring relationships in future research and evaluation, as a more viable method to assess the quality of youth mentoring programmes. Mentors are the actors with a crucial impact on the quality of the developing mentoring relationship that the intervention facilitates. Thus, it is the relationship and its quality that should be the subject of a mentoring evaluation (Brumovská, 2003; Brumovská & Seidlová Málková, 2008, 2010) to assess the quality and efficacy of formal youth mentoring interventions.

Following the "POE study", two explorative qualitative studies were conducted on mentors' perceived approach to children in formal youth mentoring relationships, to explore the nature of mentoring relationships and the principles of its benefits. In the first study (Brumovská, 2007), Czech and Swedish mentoring programmes were compared to contrast their operation and the experiences of mentors in two countries. The aim was to gain an international perspective on formal youth mentoring.

In the spring of 2007, 11 in-depth qualitative interviews (Kvale, 1996) were conducted with Czech ($n = 6$) and Swedish ($n = 5$) mentors, and with three mentoring caseworkers in two Swedish and one Czech mentoring programmes. The mentors participated in the programme for at least 1 year, were aged 21–35 years and were professional social workers or volunteers. The children were aged 9–18 years and had a range of social problems, such as loneliness, school absence, and problems with the law.

The typical Swedish mentoring programme and its operation were thus compared with the Czech BBBS programme: The Kontaktmanna Poolen with Contact Persons (CP) was chosen as a programme typical of mentoring intervention in Sweden. The mentor was a professional who became a part of the social services network with which the mentee was involved.

The programme operated as a statutory social service for socially disadvantaged youth and young offenders. Mentees were aged 13–20. They could be referred to the programme for being sentenced and have a CP compulsorily for committing a crime, or a CP was assigned to them as a support compensating their social disadvantage.

The mentors of Kontaktmanna Poolen were professional social workers and were paid a small amount for working as mentors on top of their full-time jobs. The intervention aimed to achieve concrete improvements in the youth's social problems as identified beforehand by social services. The mentoring relationship was thus oriented towards a goal of improving mentees' behaviours and was agreed with mentees and other social services at the start of the contract. The mentoring roles were rather formal and were defined clearly from the beginning to the end of the contract.

Following the analysis of the Czech and Swedish mentoring programme's operation, the same study also analysed mentors' roles in mentoring relationships, the approach styles of mentors and features of relationships that mentors developed. It also discussed mentors' dilemmas in their role. The analysis concluded (Brumovská, 2007) that regardless of the different cultural, policy, and organisational contexts of mentoring interventions, the principles and benefits of mentoring remained in the quality of experience in relationships that mentors developed with the vulnerable children and young people to support them (Brumovská, 2007).

The second qualitative study conducted in the BBBS CZ programme, between 2007 and 2010, was a content analysis (Elo & Kyngas, 2007) of the records of interviews with mentors who participated monthly in group supervision meetings for mentors, organised by the BBBS CZ/Pět P programme. The researchers compiled the records of interviews with ten mentors who were present at the meetings every month over 12 months of their mentoring involvement. The interviews were led by the programme's supervisor – a clinical or child psychologist – and recorded by the programme's caseworkers.

The researcher had access to this data when volunteering for the programme in 2000–2003 as the records of supervisions were made accessible to all volunteers present at the meetings at the time and the BBBS management team supported its use for the research. In addition to the written records of interviews, the researcher observed the interviews with mentors selected for the analysis, their matches, and their progress over the 12 months, as she also participated as a volunteer in the supervision meetings.

The data were analysed using so-called content analysis (Elo & Kyngas, 2007) in themes of relationship characteristics and dynamics perceived by mentors, and according to the mentoring literature to date. The dynamics of relationships developed according to the themes common to all tracked matches (Brumovská & Seidlová Málková, 2010, 2008). In short, the

Table 7.1 Stages and themes in the dynamics of formal youth mentoring relationships

Stage of the relationship	Common mentoring themes
Before the match	**Expectations** of mentors before the first meeting.
Months 1–2	**First impressions:** Experiences of the first meetings. Quality of the initial connection with the child from the mentor's perspective.
Months 3–5	**Getting to know each other:** Questioning and defining the contents of mentoring interactions and roles; intentions to establish a mutual connection in mentoring activities; testing and negotiating the boundaries in the interactions between a mentor and the child; coping strategies on challenging behaviour of the child.
Months 5–8	**Satisfaction** in relationships.
After 8 months	**Further dynamics** of relationships.

relationships were tracked and analysed in the relational dynamics according to the themes that each of the relational stages addressed (see Table 7.1). In other words, the themes that mentors addressed in the supervision meetings over 12 months changed and thus defined the relational dynamics. The analysis concluded that the identified themes of each relational stage are common to all tracked mentors. As a result, the stages of mentoring relationships, and the related themes of each relational stage were identified.

All the ten relationships observed throughout the study were divided according to these common themes and the differences in mentors' experiences and approaches to these. As a result, three types of mentoring relationships, with their characteristics and dynamics over 12 months, were identified: 1. Relationships with a Friendly–Equal Approach; 2. Relationships with Dilemmas of Mentors in the Mentoring Role; 3. Relationships with Authoritative–Intentional Approach of Mentors (Brumovská & Seidlová Málková, 2010, 2008):

Relationships with a friendly equal approach – Three volunteers with Friendly–Equal approaches initially felt confident about the mentoring role and had positive expectations of the personality of the mentee and future relationships. They said they connected with their mentee quickly and thoroughly during the first meeting of the match. Following that, they developed the role of a friend with a respectful and friendly approach towards mentees. They involved themselves in activities mutually with the child and thus shared experiences of play with them. After five months of involvement, these mentors were satisfied with the bond they had developed with the children, experienced the children as non-problematic, and engaged with their behaviours. Contact was maintained on a regular basis. The relationships continued beyond the formal contract with the BBBS programme after ten months of mentoring involvement.

Relationships with dilemmas of mentors in the mentoring role –
Four mentors with Dilemmas expressed doubts about their acceptance by future mentees before the meetings started. They described developing a slow initial connection with children during the first four meetings of the match. They then established two variations of the mentoring role: Firstly, mentors in the role of rescuer intended to save the child from the "evil" of the risk environment, preferably emphasizing mentees' needs regardless of their enjoyment of the mentoring meetings. Secondly, mentors in the role of observer facilitated activities but did not involve themselves in play with the child. Instead, they observed children playing on their own. After 5 months of involvement, they reported that the children started to skip the meetings intentionally or unintentionally. The children's behaviour was then interpreted as unengaged. Thus, mentors had to deal with personal dissatisfaction with the role and with the nature of the bond they developed with the children. In particular, they doubted whether the children appreciated their effort and the support they tried to offer and felt dissatisfied because they did not perceive enough appreciation from them. They also had difficulty connecting with children emotionally and looked for ways to become closer. Most of these relationships terminated at the end of the formal contract after 10 months of involvement. Mentors' feedback on the experience was described as doubtful on its meaning. Those who continued into the second year showed intentions to change the character of their involvement and to be more satisfied in the mentoring role.

Relationships with authoritative intentional approach of mentors –
Three mentors with the Authoritative–Intentional Approach had particular and concrete ideas about the character of the future mentees before the meetings started. They established goals to be achieved after 10 months as a result of their mentoring involvement. After the first mentoring meeting, they expressed a negative first impression on the connection with the child. In particular, they doubted if the child accepted them as a friend. They then developed the role of a strict, authoritative parent, trying to discipline mentees towards the norms they respected. The matches terminated prematurely before 8 months of mentoring involvement.

In sum, the early Czech studies on the BBBS CZ/Pět P youth mentoring programmes and relationships showed the need for exploration and better in-depth understanding of the principles of mentoring in the assessment of the mentoring programme's quality and benefits. The conclusion of the studies thus naturally recommended to further explore mentoring experience, its content, and its quality perceived by the mentoring participants.

As a result, following the early studies on mentoring in the BBBS CZ programme, an in-depth longitudinal qualitative tracking study was conducted in the same programme with its two affiliates in the Czech Republic. We argued for and conceptualised mentoring as being a social phenomenon. We argued that mentoring needs to be explored as the experience of mentoring participants and their qualities and dynamics to evaluate mentoring programmes' conditions and benefits. Thus, this research study was designed in the constructivist paradigm, which considers each mentoring experience and its perceived benefits to be a valuable and legitimate outcome of mentoring intervention (Brumovská, 2017).

A constructivist worldview is manifested in a phenomenological approach to research inquiry that methodologically describes and explores a person's experiences of phenomena (Creswell, 2013; Smith et al., 2012). In particular, the phenomenological approach to interviews and the IPA that was applied to data analysis describe people's lived experiences of a particular phenomenon: *what* they experienced in respect to the phenomenon under study, and *how* they experienced it (Creswell, 2013; Smith et al., 2012). The approach particularly compares and contrasts people's experiences of phenomena. It selects and collects data from people who have different experiences of the given phenomena, to attempt to describe the "universal essence" of the phenomena (Creswell, 2013; Smith et al., 2012).

The study thus aimed to explore the experiences and understandings of mentoring phenomena as mentoring participants experienced it. Fieldwork and data collection took place in two affiliates of the BBBS CZ programme in the Czech Republic from 2010 to 2012. Eleven mentoring matches were tracked for 12 months. Children, mentors, parents, and caseworkers in two BBBS CZ affiliates were interviewed on their mentoring experiences during the first month and after months four and eight of their involvement. The IPA applied to the data was conducted according to the method (Smith et al., 2012) in several hermeneutic cycles, where the data were examined, analysed, and compared. The following themes of mentors' experience were common to all 10 matches tracked over 12 months. In other words, all mentors had in common over 12 months of mentoring involvement and emphasised the following themes in their mentoring experience (Brumovská, 2017):

1 The initial motivation for volunteering
2 Perceived competence in coping with mentoring challenges
3 Perceived initial dynamics of mentoring relationships after the first month of involvement
4 Mentors' helping attitudes in the perception of the function of the mentoring role for children and perceived children's needs
5 Characteristics of collaboration and provided social supports in mentoring interactions

6 Perceived satisfaction in the mentoring role and dynamics of the relationship after 4 and 8 months of involvement
7 Perceived benefits of mentoring involvement

Although the themes were common to all participants, the study identified significant differences in tracked participants' understanding of the mentoring role, attitudes to mentees, and mentoring style. As a result, it identified the characteristics and features of FYMRs that facilitate the benefits of mentoring and thus contribute to a child's positive development and well-being. It also identified the characteristics and features and their development in FYMRs that impose potential risks on mentees. Finally, it showed mentors' motivation for volunteering and its impact on the quality and dynamics of FYMRs (Brumovská, 2017). In particular, using the self-determination theory (Ryan & Deci, 2000, 1985; Ryan & Solky, 1996), the 10 tracked mentoring matches were divided into two categories of developmental relationship: controlling, which induces potential risks in FYMRs insofar as it pressures the mentees to "think, feel, or behave in specific ways" (Ryan & Deci, 1985, p. 95) according to the expectations and preferences of the mentor; and autonomy-supportive relationships, which foster the development of mentees' authentic self through "acknowledgement of other's perceptions, acceptance of other's feelings, and absence of attempts to control the other's experience and behaviour" (Ryan & Solky, 1996, p. 252).

In sum, the last referred Czech study identified controlling and autonomy-supportive formal youth mentoring relationships in the detailed features and dynamics developed over 12 months of mentoring involvement that showed the qualities and risks of these, as well as the characteristics that predicted the resulted quality, risks, and dynamics of relationships in the later stages of the relational course. The results can be used by the mentoring programmes for assessment of mentoring relationships' qualities and thus for evaluation of the benefits of mentoring programmes for children.

Conclusion

In this chapter, we aimed to show that exploring formal youth mentoring relationships by implementing the qualitative interpretive approaches is very useful in addressing currently relevant issues within the field of youth mentoring.

We presented our opinion that the interpretive research perspective in which the exploration of the experience of mentoring as social phenomena and its qualities perceived by mentoring participants is a beneficial approach to the evaluation of the quality and benefits of mentoring programmes and services. By using the brief review of studies conducted on the Czech Big Brothers Big Sisters/Pět P youth mentoring programme between 2003 and 2017, we aimed to show the transformation of the interest in mentoring research. Moving from studying mentoring (especially mentoring relationships) from general hypotheses test-driven perspective to more in-depth interpretative approaches. We highly value the benefits of longitudinal designs for mentoring research – for their potential to reveal the importance of specific social (mentor-mentee) interaction characteristics for the quality of professional mentoring relationships. For current research on mentoring, we also see art-based, child-and-youth-centred participatory methods as very promising and beneficial, as these enable children and youth to express "their voice", reveal their specific contribution to the quality of mentoring relationships and describe views and experiences they live in mentoring relationships.

We hope we demonstrated that the in-depth understanding of the mentoring principles is needed in the field to assess the qualities of mentoring experiences. The shift from focusing on the outcomes of mentoring on children's behaviour to the assessment of qualities of mentoring experiences and perceived benefits opens a space to better understand the principles of mentoring phenomena and its contribution to children's healthy development and well-being. We think that more discussion on the contents and strategies of mentoring interventions is needed to navigate actions on bridging knowledge on positive principles of natural mentoring to the praxis of social and educational services for vulnerable children and youth.

Acknowledgements

Gabriela Seidlova Malkova's work on this chapter was supported by the Institutional Support for Long-term Development of Research Organizations at Charles University, Faculty of Humanities (2019) provided by The Ministry of Education, Youth and Sports of the Czech Republic.

Notes

1. The principle of the relationship in the *Odyssey* is the close, caring, and supportive connection in which the mentor functions as a role model for Telemachus. The mentor mediates his experiences, opinions, knowledge, and attitudes while caring for Telemachus's positive development during the years of his adolescence (Freedman, 1992).
2. Research on youth mentoring in the Czech Big Brothers Big Sisters programme in 2003 practically existed only in the studies conducted as students' bachelor's and master's research dissertations at the time. The term "youth mentoring" and the overview of the international research literature in the field were first introduced in the Czech context in the monograph called Mentoring: Towards the Professional Volunteering (Brumovská & Seidlová Málková, 2010).

References

Beck, U. (1992). *Risk society: Towards a new modernity*. New Delhi: Sage.
Bennetts, C. (2003). Mentoring youth: Trend and tradition. *British Journal of Guidance and Counselling, 31*(1), 63–74.

Big Brothers Big Sisters/Pět P. (2009). *Manuál pro koordinátory programu*. Unpublished handbook for case workers of BBBS CZ.
Blinn-Pike, L. (2007). The benefits associated with youth mentoring. In T. D. Allen, & L. T. Eby (Eds.), *The Blackwell handbook of mentoring: A multiple perspectives approach*. Malden, MA: Blackwell Publishing.
Brady, B., Dolan, P., & Canavan, J. (2017). He told me to calm down and all that': A qualitative study of forms of social support in youth mentoring relationships. *Child and Family Social Work*, 22(1), 266–274.
Brady, B., & O'Regan, C. (2009). Meeting the challenge of doing an RCT evaluation of youth mentoring in Ireland: A journey of mixed methods. *Journal of Mixed Methods Research*, 20(10), 265–280.
Brumovská, T. (2003). Analýza podoby a kvality mentoringového vztahu v sociálně-preventivním programu Pět P (Unpublished bachelor thesis). Prague, Czech Republic: School of Liberal Arts and Humanities, Charles University.
Brumovská, T. (2007). Mentors as mediators and significant adults: The role of mentors and their influence in the Czech and Swedish mentoring relationships. Degree report. Sweden: School of Social and Political Science, Department of Social Work, University of Gothenburg.
Brumovská, T. (2017). *Initial motivation and its impact on quality and dynamics in formal youth mentoring relationships: A phenomenological longitudinal study*. Doctoral thesis. Galway, Ireland: UNESCO Child and Family Research Centre, School of Political Science and Sociology, National University of Ireland, Galway.
Brumovská, T. (2018). *Youth-Initiated Mentoring with Arts-Based Participatory Action Research Approach: Benefits and Challenges*. Paper presented at European Mentoring Summit, Berlin, March 2018.
Brumovská, T., & Seidlová Málková, G. (2008). Typologie dynamiky mentoringového vztahu v programu Big Brothers Big Sisters/Pět P. Research report. Prague, Czech Republic: NIDM – National Institute for Children and Youth.
Brumovská, T., & Seidlová Málková, G. (2010). *Mentoring: Výchova k profesionálnímu dobrovolnictví*. Prague: Portál.
Clarke, C. (2009). Paths between positivism and interpretivism: An appraisal of Hay's via media. *Politics*, 29(1), 28–36.
Colley, H. (2003). *Mentoring for social inclusion: A critical approach to nurturing mentor relationships*. London: Routledge Falmer.
Cutrona, C. E. (2000). Social support principles for strengthening families. In J. Canavan, P. Dolan, & J. Pinkerton (Eds.), *Family support: Direction from diversity*. London: Jessica Kingsley.
Creswell, J. W. (2013). *Qualitative inquiry and research design: Choosing among five approaches*. London: Sage.
De Singly, F. (1999). *Sociologie současné rodiny*. Praha: Portál.
Dolan, P., & Brady, B. (2012). *A guide to youth mentoring: Providing effective social support*. London: Jessica Kingsley.
Dolan, P., Brady, B., O'Regan, C., Brumovská, T., Canavan, J., & Forcan, C. (2010). *Big brothers big sisters (BBBS) of Ireland: Report 2 – Qualitative evidence*. Galway, Ireland: Child and Family Research Centre, NUI Galway, On Behalf of Foróige.
Dolan, P., Brady, B., O'Regan, C., Russell, D., Canavan, J., & Forcan, C. (2011). *Big brothers big sisters of Ireland report: Randomised control trial and implementation report*. Galway, Ireland: Child and Family Research Centre, NUI Galway, On Behalf of Foróige.

DuBois, D. L., Holloway, B. E., Valentine, J. C., & Cooper, H. (2002). Effectiveness of mentoring programs for youth: A meta-analytic review. *American Journal of Community Psychology*, *30*(2), 157–197.

DuBois, D. L., Portillo, N., Rhodes, J. E., Silverthorne, N., & Valentine, J. C. (2011). How effective are mentoring programs for youth? A systematic assessment of the evidence. *Psychological Science in the Public Interest*, *12*(2), 57–91.

DuBois, D.L., & Silverthorn, N. (2005). Characteristics of natural mentoring relationships and adolescent adjustment: Evidence from the national study. *Journal of Primary Prevention*, *26*(2), 69–92.

Elo, S., & Kyngas, H. (2007). The qualitative content analysis process. *Journal of Advanced Nursing*, *62*(1), 107–115.

Feuerstein, R., & Feuerstein, S. (1999). Mediated learning experience: A theoretical review. In R. Feuerstein, P. Klein, & A. J. Tannenbaum (Eds.), *Mediated learning experience (MLE): Theoretical, psychological and learning implications* (pp. 3–52). London: Freund Publishing House.

Feuerstein, R., Yaacov, R., & Rynders, J. E. (1988). *Mediated learning experience: What makes it powerful? Don't accept me as I am – Helping "retarded" people to excel* (pp. 59–93). New York, NY: Plenum Publishing Corporation.

Freedman, M. (1992). *The kindness of strangers: Reflections on the mentoring movement*. Philadelphia, PA: Public/Private Ventures.

Frič, P., & Pospíšilová, T. (2010). *Vzorce a hodnoty dobrovolnictví v české společnosti na začátku 21. století*. Praha: Agnes.

Grossman, J., & Rhodes, J. E. (2002). The test of time: Predictors and effects of duration in youth mentoring relationships. *American Journal of Community Psychology*, *30*(2), 199–219.

Hall, J. C. (2003). *Mentoring and young people: A literature review*. SCRE Research Report no. 114. Glasgow: University of Glasgow.

Javornicky, M. (2018). 'Interpretative Phenomenological Analysis as a method of interpretive sociology – philosophical case'. In: 'Resistance and mobilization of political power: The case of Irish senior citizens'. https://doi.org/10.13140/RG.2.2.33175.47529

Keller, T. E. (2007). *Youth mentoring: Theoretical and methodological issues. The Blackwell handbook of mentoring – A multiple perspective approach*. London. Blackwell Publishing.

Kraemer, H. C. (2015). Evaluating interventions. In A. Thaper, D. Pine, J. Leckman, S. Scott, M. Snowling, & E. Taylor (Eds.), *Rutter's child and adolescent psychiatry*. Oxford: Wiley.

Kvale, S. (1996). *InterViews: An introduction to qualitative research interviewing*. London: Sage.

Morrow, K.V., & Styles, M. B. (1992). *Linking lifetimes. A study of mentoring relationships in linking lifetimes mentoring program*. Philadelphia, PA: Public/Private Venture.

Morrow, K.V., & Styles, M. B. (1995). *Building a relationship with youth in programme setting: A study of big brothers big sisters*. Philadelphia, PA: Public/Private Venture.

Philip, K. (1997). 'New perspectives on mentoring: Young people, youth work and mentoring'. Unpublished PhD dissertation. The University of Aberdeen.

Programme Pět P. (2007). *Manual for caseworkers, 2007*.

Rhodes, J. E. (2005). A model of youth mentoring. In D. L. DuBois, & M. J. Karcher (Eds.), *Handbook of youth mentoring*. Thousand Oaks, CA: Sage.

Rhodes, J. E. (2018). 'Research on the quality of mentoring relationships: How to build strong relationships?' Keynote at European Mentoring Summit, Berlin, March 2018.

Rhodes, J. E., Contreras, J. M., & Mangelsdorf, S. C. (1994). Natural mentor relationships among Latina adolescent mothers: Psychological adjustment, moderating processes and the role of early parental acceptance. *American Journal of Community Psychology*, *22*, 211–228.

Rogoff, B. (1990). *Apprenticeship in thinking: Cognitive development in social context.* New York, NY: Oxford University Press.

Ryan, R. M., & Deci, E. L. (1985). *Intrinsic motivation and self-determination in human behavior.* New York, NY: Plenum Press.

Ryan, R. M., & Deci, E. L. (2000). Intrinsic and extrinsic motivations: Classic definitions and new directions. *Contemporary Educational Psychology, 25,* 54–67.

Ryan, R. M., & Solky, J. A. (1996). What is supportive about social support? On the psychological needs for autonomy and relatedness. In: G. R. Pierce, B. R. Sarason, & I. G. Sarason (Eds.), *Handbook of social support and the family* (pp. 249–267). New York, NY: Plenum Press.

Sánchez, B., Esparza, P., Berardi, L., & Pryce, J. (2011). Mentoring in the context of Latino youth's broader village during their transition to high school. *Youth and Society, 43*(1), 225–52.

Smith, J. A., Flowers, P., & Larkin, M. (2012). *Interpretive phenomenological analysis: Theory, method and research.* London: Sage.

Spencer, R. (2007). It's not what I expected: A qualitative study of youth mentoring relationships' failures. *Journal of Adolescent Research, 22*(4), 2–25.

Spencer, R., Liang, B., Rhodes, J. E., West, J., & Singer, R. (2006). Ethics in youth mentoring relationships: Where are the boundaries? *The Community Psychologist, 39*(3), 35–37.

Tierney, J., Grossman, J., & Resch, N. (1997). *Making a difference: An impact study of big brothers big sisters of America.* Philadelphia, PA: Public/Private Ventures.

Van Dam, L., Smit, D., Wildschut, B., Branje, S., Rhodes, J., Assink, M., ... Stams, G. J. (2018). Does natural mentoring matter? A three-level meta-analysis on the association between natural mentoring and youth outcomes. *American Journal of Community Psychology, 62*(1-2), 203–220.

Vygotsky, L. S. (1978). *Mind in society.* Cambridge, MA: Harvard University Press.

Werner, E. E., & Smith, R. S. (2001). *Journeys from childhood to midlife: Risk, resilience and recovery.* New York, NY: Cornell University Press.

Zand, D. H., Thomson, N., Cervantes, R., Espiritu R., & Klagholz, D. (2009). The mentor–youth alliance: The role of mentoring relationships in promoting youth competence. *Journal of Adolescence, 32*(1), 1–17.

Zimmerman, M. A., Bingerheimer, J. B., & Notaro, P. C. (2002). Natural mentors and adolescent resiliency: A study with urban youth. *American Journal of Community Psychology, 30*(2), 221–243.

Conclusions

The contributions of this book have shown the need for further reflection on how mentoring can favour the emancipation of children and young people. This debate must be accompanied by fluid and ongoing communication between academics and practitioners, taking into consideration the voice and needs of the children and youth we serve. Further, as previous studies have shown, this debate is necessary given that some well-designed and well-intentioned programmes have not achieved the expected results or have in fact brought about unwanted consequences (Rhodes, Liang, & Spencer, 2009). In this regard, we must continue working to ensure that mentoring initiatives that have been implemented from a top-down and atomising perspective take into account the needs and desires of the groups to which they are directed.

Following from these reflections, we present a **decalogue** of elements that, for us, would characterise youth-mentoring relationships from an empowering perspective. We must stress that this decalogue is intended to be a starting point for mentoring programmes to spark an internal debate, and deepen their understanding of how these elements are being worked on, and what specific practices can be developed in the future to move toward this goal. It also outlines some elements that may be linked to a future research agenda; as we need more evidence, in different contexts, to enhance knowledge in this area. Thus, mentoring programmes can move forward towards the emancipation of children and young people if they:

1 **Take into account social capital and the connections between formal and natural mentoring** – Programmes must identify, in their context, how formal mentoring can lead to informal mentoring relationships through the generation of social capital and the relationships that children and young people can establish with institutional actors or agents of empowerment in their environment (Stanton-Salazar, 2011). Generally, both formal and natural mentoring have been studied separately; however, there are still very few analyses that make it clear how the latter may be the result of the former. We must also further explore

how these relationships have a direct impact on community and civic engagement (Brady & Dolan, 2009).

2 **Encourage Youth-Initiated Mentoring** – It is necessary to take into account how the child and/or young person play a decisive role in choosing their mentors. Authors such as Schwartz, Rhodes, Spencer, and Grossman (2013) have shown how people from the young person's environment can become mentors. In this way, mentoring relationships emerge that are closer to natural mentoring. However, it should also be borne in mind that not all children and young people have access to individuals who can potentially become their mentors. From our point of view, these mentors should fulfil a series of criteria such as (a) the ability to identify systemic barriers that affect the lives of mentored youth, (b) the ability to transmit information to children and young people so that they can learn how to navigate the system and connect their interests and motivations with their studies, (c) the ability to be agents of listening and emotional support, and (d) the ability to identify other agents who may support their mentees.

3 **Establish egalitarian relationships that are mutually beneficial** – the approach of the programmes takes into account and manifests how mentoring has mutual benefits not only for mentees but also for mentors. While the development of the potential of the child and young person is always at the centre of the action, the programmes also highlight the benefits of mentoring to mentors, and they are conscious of this. This awareness and orientation can prevent markedly ethnocentrist and paternalistic mentoring relationships from occurring, which can adversely affect young people's emancipation.

4 **Take a comprehensive view of the social inclusion of mentees rather than one based on the deficiencies or shortcomings they may have** – In this regard, Lerner (2004) emphasises the need for programmes that support adolescents and young people, and that focus on developing positive and sustained relationships between them and the adults around them in order to enhance their competencies. At times, some programmes have emphasised the disadvantages of the youth they serve, rather than focusing their efforts on creating spaces and relationships that nurture their development and emphasise their potential.

5 **Develop critical awareness of existing inequalities and promote social change** – On this issue, there have been many authors who, using Freirean logic, have emphasised the need for mentors to foster not only the empowerment of children and young people, but also the development of a critical consciousness of the world they live in (Stanton-Salazar, 2011). In this vein, Liang, Spencer, West, and Rappaport (2013) also stressed the need for mentoring relationships to not only be connected to individual change but to social change as well. That is, for mentoring

programmes to promote an orientation based on social justice, and to define both the purpose of mentoring relationships and how they contribute to creating active citizens for a better world.

6 **Promote a set of recursive dynamics that can be used in meetings between the mentoring pair and in the achievement of their established objectives** – Mentoring programmes can offer a range of recursive dynamics, as Rhodes (2018, March) points out, to promote the acquisition of non-cognitive or socio-emotional skills in children and young people in connection with the objectives of these programmes. To make this possible, mentors need to be selected who have these teaching skills, but we also must identify the interactions and practices that can have the greatest effect on mentees, based on the goals of the programme. With this information, programmes can better target the training of their mentors and monitor them more accurately. For example, recent research carried out in Spain with adolescent mentees of immigrant origin showed that certain group activities favoured a greater acquisition of language competencies and social skills (University of Girona, 2018–2020). This and similar evidence can help mentoring programmes to create this portfolio of resources through which they can more accurately train their mentors and promote more effective mentoring.

7 **Make significant and relevant connections (attunement) between the spaces of mentoring relationships (informal support) and the welfare system (formal support)** – Mentoring is not a substitute for the welfare state's responsibilities. Although there may be different welfare state regimes depending on the context (Esping-Andersen, 1990), the informal support provided by mentors should be complementary to public policies and the formal support of educational and social professionals. In this regard, it is important to observe how mentoring programmes can collaborate with professionals in these fields in order to complement each other.

8 **Focus more on the quality of mentoring relationships rather than the quantity** – Some programmes emphasise the need to promote as many mentoring relationships as possible. This dynamic is often reflected in the entities' annual reports, when they explicitly state the growing number of mentoring relationships they have established in recent years. Sometimes the reason that drives organisations into this dynamic of growth or expansion is determined by funding bodies and is often linked to the misconception that mentoring relationships, in and of themselves, generate improved social welfare for children and young people, and thus the more the better. In this respect, the data from different meta-analyses (DuBois, Portillo, Rhodes, Silverthorn, & Valentine, 2011; Raposa et al., 2019) shows that while there are mentoring programmes that have a significant impact, there are others that do not, and that some may even have a negative effect on mentees. Therefore, in

future years we will have to work – more in depth – and clarify what we mean by quality mentoring programmes. It is quite likely that this word may be polysemous; there may be different interpretations of what is meant by quality, or this may vary depending on the context. This book has provided some elements that can help in this debate regarding the emancipation of children and young people through mentoring.

9 **Consider the relationships with the child's or young person's family and their community** – Often, it is assumed that mentoring sessions should occur outside the neighbourhood or environment of the child and/or young person because "the neighbourhood or the environment in which they live is stigmatised". While it is sometimes important to leave the neighbourhood to accompany them to experience resources and institutions that they often do not have access to (e.g. museums, university campuses, discovering the city, etc.), it is also crucial for mentors to be comfortable in the context where the child or young person has built their everyday life – interacting and establishing trusting relationships with their parents, family, and community. Insight into how these programmes work on these synergies and relationships, and how they affect children and young people, will be vital in the years to come.

10 **Define the objectives of the programme together with the groups they serve**: Often, the objectives of the programmes are defined by the organisation that runs them or by their funders (be it a government agency or a philanthropic entity). Generally, they seek to address a socially constructed social problem, and see mentoring as a useful and supportive tool for people living in this disadvantaged situation. However, if programmes and funders want to promote more inclusive objectives and approaches, the voices of potential participants and their families should be considered when analysing whether their concerns are the same, and if the approach and objectives emerge from a dialogue between the different agents involved.

References

Brady, B., & Dolan, P. (2009). Youth mentoring as a tool for community and civic engagement: Reflections on findings of an Irish research study. *Community Development*, 40(4), 359–366.

DuBois, D. L., Portillo, N., Rhodes, J. E., Silverthorn, N., & Valentine, J. C. (2011). How effective are mentoring programs for youth? A systematic assessment of the evidence. *Psychological Science in the Public Interest*, 12(2), 57–91.

Esping-Andersen, G. (1990). *The three worlds of welfare capitalism*. Cambridge: Polity Press.

Lerner, R. M. (2004). *Liberty: Thriving and civic engagement among America's youth*. Thousand Oaks, CA: Sage.

Liang, B., Spencer, R., West, J., & Rappaport, N. (2013). Expanding the reach of youth mentoring: Partnering with youth for personal growth and social change. *Journal of Adolescence*, 36, 257–267.

Raposa, E. B., Rhodes, J. E., Stams, G. J. J. M., Card, N., Burton, S., Schwartz, S., … Hussain, S. (2019). The effects of youth mentoring programs: A meta-analysis of outcome studies. *Journal of Youth and Adolescence, 48*(3), 423–443.

Rhodes, J. E. (2018, March). *Research on quality of mentoring relationships: How to build strong relationships.* [Video file]. Retrieved from https://mentoringsummit.eu/speakers/jean-rhodes/

Rhodes, J., Liang, B., & Spencer, R. (2009). First do no harm: Ethical principles for youth mentoring relationships. *Professional Psychology: Research and Practice, 40*(5), 452–458.

Schwartz, S. E. O., Rhodes, J. E., Spencer, R., & Grossman, J. B. (2013). Youth initiated mentoring: Investigating a new approach to working with vulnerable adolescents. *American Journal of Community Psychology, 52*(1–2) 155–169.

Stanton-Salazar, R. D. (2011). A social capital framework for the study of institutional agents and their role in the empowerment of low-status students and youth. *Youth & Society, 43*(3), 1066–1109.

University of Girona. (2018–2020). *Applying mentoring: Social and technological innovations for the social inclusion of migrants and refugees.* Retrieved from http://mentoringapp.vahid.es/en/

Index

Note: *Italicized* page numbers refer to figures, **bold** numbers indicate tables and page numbers with "n" indicate endnote.

ability: Connexions 20; to cope with stress 67; to identify social inequalities 5; to identify systemic barriers 129; mentee 47; mentors 5; social entities 96
academic achievement 42, 53
academic challenges 54
academic integration 53
academic outcomes 99
academic success 53
accepted position 80
achievement 4; academic 42, 53; goals 70; indicators 99; objectives 130
activism *see* community activism; social activism
additive effects approach 98; *see also* approaches
adolescence/adolescents 9, 36, 41–42, 52–53, 57, 59, 64–65, 67–68, 71, 87, 97, 99–100, 104–107, 129
adults: critical consciousness (CC) 35–37; mentors 32, 59; non-parental 16, 34–38, 42, 48–49, 67–69, 87, 97
anchors *see* mentor(s)
anti-social behaviours 104, 113; *see also* behaviours
approaches: to natural mentoring 56–58; to recruit mentors 50; youth mentoring 48–50; *see also* presence approach
assessment 110–124; Czech mentoring intervention programme 116–123; formal youth mentoring interventions 112–116; formal youth mentoring research 111–112; mentees 118; Multiple Social Support Attunement (MSSA) 98–100; natural mentoring 111–112
attentive listening 26–27
attitudes: help-seeking 54, 56; skills and 48, 50, 54, 59; students 54, 56
Austria 2
autonomy *see* critical autonomy
awareness *see* critical awareness

Baart, A. 16–17, 26, 28–29
BBBS CZ/Pět P 117, 119, 121–122
BBBS International 117
behaviours: anti-social 104, 113; covert and overt 71; juveniles disruptive 84; problem 42, 65, 71; prosocial 104; rule-breaking 87
beliefs *see* negative beliefs
belonging *see* sense of belonging
Beresford, P. 19
Big Brothers Big Sisters of America (BBBSA) 21–22, 24–25, 33, 48, 114
bioecological model 95–97
Blair, T. 11
Blakeslee, J. E. 9
bonding social capital 4; *see also* social capital
Bourdieu, P. 3–4
Brady, B. 19–21
Brazil 34
bridging social capital 4; *see also* social capital

Cameron, D. 11
Canada 48
Canadian Mentoring Partnership 11
candidate status 80
capital *see* specific capital
Caregiver Initiated Mentoring 57, 59

Catlett, B. S. 40
Cavell, T. A. 6
challenges: academic 54; adolescence 97; cultural 2; faced by children 1–2; in formal and informal mentoring 51; of networking 55
Ching, D. 58
coevolution 96–97
cognitive behavioural therapy (CBT) 83
cognitive skills 112; *see also* skills
Coleman, J. S. 3–4
collaboration with social networks 68–69
college students 32, 34, 38–40, 53–56, 59
Colley, H. 11, 20
community activism 40
complex needs 52, 67–68, 87; *see also* needs
complex systems theory 100
connectedness: help-seeking and 58; school 36; well-being and 47; youth-adult 50, 59
Connected Scholars 6, 48, 53–56, 59
Connexions 20
conscientização *see* critical consciousness (CC)
consciousness *see* critical consciousness (CC)
consideration and invitation 77–78
Contact Persons (CP) 118–119
content analysis 119
Convention on the Rights of the Child 66
covert and overt behaviours 71; *see also* behaviours
critical action 42
critical autonomy: children and young people 11–12; defined 1; development 2; social capital 7, 9, 11–12
critical awareness 129–130
critical consciousness (CC) 10, 32–43; adults 35–37; critical perspective 32–33; defined 32; development among college students 38–40; mentoring 32–43; mentors 36; research 40–43
critical perspective 32–33
critical reflection 42
critical thinking 5
cultural capital 2–4, 54
cultural heritage 29
Czech Big Brothers Big Sisters/Pět P 110, 116, 123
Czech mentoring intervention programme 116–123

decalogue 128
decision-making 17, 20, 36, 42, 68–70
deficit-based paradigm 48; *see also* positivist paradigm
de Goias, R. 2
delinquent behaviour 52; *see also* behaviours
Diemer, M. A. 35
dignity 28–29
Dolan, P. 19–21
Doyal, L. 1

economic capital 2–4
economic inequalities 40
egalitarian relationships 129; *see also* relationships
Elledge, L. C. 6
employability 20
empowerment 47–60; approaches to natural mentoring relationships 56–58; approaches to recruit mentors 50; children and young people 3, 7; Connected Scholars 53–56; formal approaches to youth mentoring 48–50; paradigm change 7; social capital 5–7; theory and research 34; well-being and 1; Youth-Initiated Mentoring (YIM) 51–53
engagement mentoring 11; *see also* mentoring
Erskine, R. 101
ethnicity 49
Europe 1, 111–112
European Commission 12
Everyday Mentoring 57–59; *see also* mentoring
Eye Movement Desensitization and Reprocessing (EMDR) 83
Eyler, J. 39

feedback 36, 55, 82, 96, 121
Feuerstein, R. 111–112
footing 80
formal mentoring 47, 69, 128–129; *see also* mentoring
formal support 107, 130
formal youth mentoring: interventions 112–116; relationships 112, **120**, 123; research 111–112; *see also* youth mentoring
foster care 21, 24, 66
Freire, P. 5, 35, 42

gender 21, 49, 51, 105
Giles, D. E., Jr. 39
Gough, I. 1
Gouthro, S. 2
grade point average (GPA) 55–56
Granovetter, M. 4
Great Britain 11, 48
Green, A. E. 39
Grossman, J. B. 129
growth in personal environment (GRIP) study 88

habitus 8, 11
help-seeking: attitudes 54, 56; connectedness and 58
hierarchy 96–97
high-attuned multiple social support 102, *103*, 105; see also Multiple Social Support Attunement (MSSA)
high school students 6, 40, 55, 59; see also students
Hoadley, C. 58
Homer 111
Hughes, K. L. 54

immigrants 1–2, 4
improvisation, MSSA 101–102, *103*, 106
inclusion 5, 7, 11, 17, 129
InConnection team 69
individual-focused paradigm 48
inequalities 5, 40, 129–130
informal mentor 82; see also mentor(s)
informal mentoring 68–69; see also mentoring
informal mentors 57–58, 65, 83; see also mentor(s)
informal support 6, 130
institutional agents 5, **8**, 8–9, 53
Intentional Mentoring 57–59
interactive effects 99–100
interactive effects approach 98; see also approaches
interpretive paradigm 115–116
Interpretive Phenomenological Analysis (IPA) 116, 122
interventions, youth mentoring 110–124
invitation see consideration and invitation
Ireland 21–22, 114
Israel 48

Junior Cert 23, 29n1
juveniles 64, 68, 76, 78, 83–84, 87

Karp, M. M. 54
Keij, J. 79
Keller, T. E. 9
Kontaktmanna Poolen 118–119
Kuis, E. E. 17–18, 26–28

labour market 4, 11
la Coordinadora de Mentoría Social 11
Larose, S. 100
learning see mediated learning; mutual learning
Leaving Certificate 23, 29n1
Lerner, R. M. 129
Levinas, E. 79
Li, C. H. 35
Liang, B. 9, 35, 129
Life Chances Strategy campaign 11
lifestyles 8
linguistic capital 1–2
listening see attentive listening
longitudinal research 67–68, 106; see also research
low-attuned multiple social support 102, *103*; see also Multiple Social Support Attunement (MSSA)
low-income Latino youth 5

marketization 19
McGregor, C. 19–21
mediated learning 111
mentees: ability 47; access to networks and contacts 8; assessment 118; development 111; mentors and 5, 16, 35, 94, 98; natural network 9–10; needs 20; skills 7, 111; social inclusion of 129; see also mentor(s)
MENTOR 11
mentor(s) 2; ability 5; adult 32, 59; approaches to recruit 50; critical consciousness (CC) 9, 36; dilemmas in mentoring role 121; egocentric network 9–10; emotional support 2; experience 122–123; goals 20; mentees and 5, 16, 35, 94, 98; micro-level **8**; micro-level of 9–10; motivation 117; as presence practitioners 26; protégés and 7, 9–10; psychosocial support 2; recruitment 47–60; selection 10; social justice training for 40; social worker and 20; training 36; training and support 10; volunteer 51; see also mentees; presence approach

mentoring: critical consciousness (CC) 32–43; gap 13; learning and 38–40; meso-level **8**; organisations **8**, 10; process 114; relationships 130–131; social capital 3–12, **8**; social change 32–43; sociopolitical context 11–12; volunteer relationships 35
mentor-mentee relationships 9, 19
meta-analysis 2, 49, 64, 68
Mexico 48
middle-class undergraduate students 40; *see also* students
middle-school students 39, 57; *see also* students
motivation 5, 10, 65, 70, 73, 129; mentors 117; network 74–77; students 37; Youth-Initiated Mentoring (YIM) 65–67
MSSA *see* Multiple Social Support Attunement (MSSA)
multi-level framework, social capital 7–12, **8**
Multiple Social Support Attunement (MSSA) 94–107; assessment trends in 98–100; described 100–103, *103*; example 102–103; social relationships 95–98; stages 102–103; well-being 105; youth development 95–98; youth social development 103–105
mutual learning 9

National Guard Youth ChalleNGe Program (NGYCP) 52
National Mentoring Partnership 11
natural mentoring 35, 47, 50, 56–59, 64–65, 69, 87, 110–113, 115, 124, 128–129; *see also* mentoring
natural mentoring relationship (NMR) 110–112
needs 27–28; adolescents 65; child 117; complex 52, 67–68, 87; family 69, 77; mentees 20, 36, 72, 121; mentors 9, 72; target group 20; young people 20, 27–28; youth 98, 106
negative beliefs 54
negative social interactions 67
Netherlands 17, 64–88
network motivation 74–77
network orientation 56
New York 5–6
New Zealand 48
New Zealand Youth Mentoring Network 11

non-cognitive skills 130; *see also* skills
non-parental adults 16, 34–38, 42, 48–49, 67–69, 87, 97
North America 34

Odyssey (Homer) 111
OECD 12
O'Gara, L. 54
openness 96
out-of-home placements 66, 69, 87
overt behaviours *see* covert and overt behaviours

paradigm change 7, 12
partial improvisation, MSSA 102
participatory action research 42; *see also* research
Pathways of Benefits in FYMRs 112
Peppler, K. 58
perceived social support 67
perceptions 3, 8, 54, 99–100, 104, 113, 123
performance, MSSA 101–102, *103*
perspective *see* critical perspective
Philip, K. 20
political efficacy 34
positioning theory 80
positivist paradigm 113
practical matters 83
Prague 117
praxis 42, 110, 112–113, 124
presence approach 16–29; case studies 22–25; concept 17–18; principles 18; youth mentoring 18–22, 26; *see also* approaches
presence practitioners 17–18, 26–28; *see also* mentor(s)
problem-posing education 35
problem-solving 17, 27–29, 111
Programme-Based Outcome Evaluation (POE) 117–118
programmes objectives 131
programme staff 10
Progressive Era 48
Project DREAM 57, 59
prosocial behaviour 104; *see also* behaviours
protégés 2–3; family or tutors of 9; mentor and 7, 9–10; personal agenda 11
Proweller, A. 40
psychological problems 71
psychological stress 67

psychology 2; *see also* social psychology
Putnam, R. 4–5

qualitative research 12
quality: mentoring relationships 130–131; relationships 16, 18
quantitative research 12

race/ethnicity 49
racial inequalities 40
Raithelhuber, E. 2
randomised control trial (RCT) 113–114, 117–118
Rappaport, N. 129
recruitment, mentors 47–60
recursive dynamics 7, 12, 130
reflection *see* critical reflection
refugees 1–2
rehearsal, MSSA 101–102, *103*
relationships 131; approaches to natural mentoring 56–58; with authoritative intentional approach of mentors 121; with dilemmas of mentors in mentoring role 121; egalitarian 129; formal youth mentoring 112, **120**, 123; with friendly equal approach 120; mentoring 130–131; mentor-mentee 9, 19; quality 16, 18; staff-youth 36; supportive 47, 67–68; youth-adult 42
research: Connected Scholars 55; critical consciousness (CC) 40–43; Czech mentoring intervention programme 116–123; youth mentoring 111–112; *see also* specific research
residential care 21
resiliency 111, 113, 115
Rhodes, J. E. 7, 19, 112, 114, 129–130
robustness 96–97
Rueger, S. Y. 99
rule-breaking behaviours 87; *see also* behaviours
Rynders, J. E. 111

Santo, R. 58
school principals, role 37
Schwartz, S. E. O. 129
Scottish Mentoring Network 11
self-assessment 118; *see also* assessment
self-determination theory 123
self-efficacy 34, 55
self-evaluation 17–18
self-organisation 96–97

self-regulation 104
sense of belonging 2
service learning 34, 38–41
shared decision-making 68, 70; *see also* decision-making
Shier, M. L. 2
skills: attitudes and 48, 50, 54, 59; mentee 7, 111; problem-solving 111
Small, M. L. 5–6, 10
Smith, R. C. 10
soapbox 82–83
sociability 2–3
social action participation 37
social activism 35, 42
social barriers 9
social capital 1–13, 53–56, 106, 128–129; children and young people 11–12; critical autonomy 7, 9, 11–12; defined 4; empowerment 6–7; mentoring 3–12, **8**; multi-level framework 7–12, **8**; sociability and 3; social inequality and 10; types 4; well-being and 6
social care 18–19
social change 9, 32–43, 129–130
social development 94–107, 103–105
social entities 96
social exclusion 4
social inclusion 7; of children and young people 12; of mentees 129
social inequality 1, 5, 9–10, 38
social integration 53, 67
social interaction 112
socialization 5
social justice 36, 40
social learning 111
social loafing 68
social networks 65, 67–69, 73, 82, 88, 106
social psychology 68
social skills 103, 130
social stimulation 67
social supports 29, 67, 99, 115
social worker 18–19; mentors and 20; teachers and 20
socio-emotional skills 130
sociopolitical control 34, 36–37
Soucy, N. 100
Spain 130
Spencer, R. 52, 129
Spratt, J. 20
staff-youth relationships 36; *see also* relationships
Stanton-Salazar, R. 4–5

strengths 28–29
stress 10, 24, 26, 67, 84, 113, 128
students 53–56; academic performance 56; academic success 53; attitudes 54, 56; college 32, 34, 38–40, 53–56, 59; of colour 37; high school 6, 40, 55, 59; middle-class undergraduate 40; middle-school 39, 57; motivation 37; service-learning 38–39; skills 55; university 4, 6
substance use 42
support *see* formal support; informal support
supportive relationships 47, 64, 67–68
Sweden 118
systemic inequality 39
systems theory 96, 100
system therapy 83

teachers 7, 9–10, 20, 35, 37, 58, 64, 97, 99–100, 102–104; *see also* mentor(s)
thinking *see* critical thinking
Tierney, J. 117–118
top-down process 68–69
totality 96–97
treatment-as-usual (TAU) 55

Uganda 22
unattuned multiple social support 102
UNESCO 12
UNICEF 12
United States 1–2, 32–33, 37, 47–60, 112, 114, 117
university students 4, 6; *see also* students
unpredictability 96

values 33, 37, 95–97, 101, 111
Varga, S. M. 97–98
violence prevention 40
volunteer mentors 51; *see also* mentor(s)
Vygotsky, L. S. 111–112

well-being 94–107; connectedness and 47; empowerment and 1; health and 111; Multiple Social Support Attunement (MSSA) 105; positive development and 123; social capital and 6
West, J. 129
World Bank 12

Yaacov, R. 111
youth-adult partnerships 35–36
youth-adult relationships 42
youth development 95–98, 103–105
Youth-Initiated Mentoring (YIM) 6, 8, 10, 48, 51–53, 56, 59, 64–88, 129; dilemma 79; effectiveness 74–75, 87–88; embedded in treatment context 69–70; encouragement 129; impact and position of 78–82; motivation 65–67; phases 70–83, 71; theoretical background 67–83; working with 83–86, **85–86**
youth mentoring 16; assessment of quality 110–124; defined 47; formal approaches to 48–50; interventions 110–124; Multiple Social Support Attunement (MSSA) 94–107; presence approach 18–22, 26; research 111–112; risks 39
youth social development 103–105

Zaff, J. F. 97–98